ONE HUNDRED
LOVE LETTERS
FOR GOD'S WOMEN

PART TWO

ONE HUNDRED
LOVE LETTERS
FOR GOD'S WOMEN

PART TWO

Minister Ingrid S. Rennie

ISBN:	Hardcover	978-1-4500-7036-2
	Softcover	978-1-4500-7035-5

This book was printed in the United States of America.

To order additional copies of this book, contact:
Xlibris Corporation
1-888-795-4274
www.Xlibris.com
Orders@Xlibris.com
48807

Contents

Introduction!

These Love Letters are an expression of love directly from Father's heart to yours.

They serve as a reminder of how much He really loves you through His Son Jesus. They are also to remind you to love Him with all your heart, soul, mind and strength, while being reminded that He is your first love. He will never leave nor forsake you, nor will He ever break covenant with you (Deuteronomy 6:5).

They also serve as a reminder to make Him "Priority Number One," in your daily life by drawing close to Him, so He can draw closer to you.

They will remind you that the Lord TRULY is the greatest lover of your soul, as He is really concerned about your eternal soul.

These Love Letters comes directly from the throne room of God. They are all scriptures taken from the Holy Bible, and written in the form of Love Letters. They bring joy, comfort, peace and hope to the heart of every woman who reads them.

They can be used as a daily devotion because they are filled with words of wisdom, encouragement and direction for daily life, and life's situations. They are loaded with knowledge and insight for living, and they will give you a desire to come to know the Lord better, and motivate you to read the BIBLE, which is your basic instruction for life before leaving the earth.

Love Letters can also be used as a teaching tool, for sharing with others, just sharing the love of the Father through His son Jesus, or when you just want to receive a personal word from the Lord!

My prayer is that the Lord will give you revelation knowledge of His great, unconditional, everlasting love for you as you read these love letters!

Blessings and victory to you as you receive these love letters and allow Father to minister to you through His all powerful word, in Jesus name!

♥ BE ENCOURAGED TODAY MY LOVE ♥

My love,

My precious daughter, I want you to listen to the teachings of Jesus and build your life on the solid foundation, and as you begin to put My word into practice they will make you wise, so when the rain comes down and the streams rise, and the winds blow and beat against your house it will not fall, because you have built your life on the rock, "JESUS," however, if you hear these words of Mine, and does not put them into practice, you will be like a foolish person who built their house on the sand, so when the rain comes down, and the streams rise, and the winds blow and beat against your house, it will fall with a great crash.

My love, I want you to understand and follow My instructions, and you My love will enjoy a life of prosperity and success, be reminded that those who are willing and obedient will eat the good of the land, so don't just listen to My word, you must do what it says; otherwise, you are only fooling yourself. For if you listen to the word and don't obey it; it is like glancing at your face in a mirror. You see yourself, walk away, and forget what you look like. But if you look carefully into the perfect law that sets you free, and if you do what it says, and don't forget what you have heard, then I will bless you for doing it.

My love, I also want you to learn to exercise your faith in Me, and My promises made to you. I want you to understand that faith is being sure of what you hope for, and certain of what you do not see. This is what the ancients were commended for. My love, My precious daughter, I want you to trust Me with all of your heart, do not lean on your own understanding, but acknowledge Me in all of your ways and I will direct your path, and be reminded that those who trust in Me are as secure as Mount Zion; they will not be defeated but will endure forever, for just as the mountains surround Jerusalem, I surrounds My people, all those who have built confident trust in Me through My written word.

So I encourage you My love, to purpose in your heart to become a true worshiper, one who would worship Me in spirit and truth, love Me with all your heart, soul, mind and strength. Seek first My kingdom and righteousness, and make Me priority number One in your life! Learn to answer the call to worship, and worship Me in Spirit and truth My love.

(Matt 7:24-27; Joshua1:8; Hebrews11:1-3; Proverbs3:5&6)!

Love,

Make Me your priority Number One

POINTS TO CONSIDER

1. Build your life on the solid foundation of God's word.

2. Put the word into practice for your life, it will make you wise.

3. Learn to exercise your faith it will keep you strong.

4. Be reminded that your obedience guarantees great benefits.

5. Follow Father's instructions and you will enjoy a life of prosperity and success.

6. Don't just listen to the word; you must do what it says. Otherwise, you are only fooling yourself.

7. Make the Lord Priority number One in your life.

❤❤ *BE ENCOURAGED TODAY MY LOVE* ❤❤

❤❤

My Love,

I have searched you and I know everything about you. I know when you sit and when you rise; I perceive your thoughts from afar.

I discern your going out and your lying down, and I Am familiar with all your ways. Before a word is on your tongue I know it completely. I hem you in—behind and before, and I have laid My hand upon you. Such knowledge is too wonderful for you, too much for you to understand.

You can never go from My Spirit; you cannot flee from My presence.

If you go up to heaven, I Am there; if you make your bed in the depths, I Am there. If you rise on the wings of the dawn, if you settle on the far side of the sea, even there My hand will guide you, My right hand will hold you steadfast.

My love, If you say, "Surely the darkness will hide me, and the light become night around you," even the darkness will not be dark to Me; because the night shines like the day, for darkness is as light to Me.

Be reminded My love, that I created your inmost being and I knitted you together in your mother's womb; you are fearfully and wonderfully made; My works are wonderful, you need to understand that My love!

Your frame was not hidden from Me when I made you in the secret place, when I weaved you together in the depths of the earth. My love, My eyes saw your unformed body. All the days ordained for you were written in My book before one of them came to be, how precious you are to Me.

My love, My thoughts towards you are very great. If you were to count them they would outnumber the grains of sand on the seashore, and when you awake, I Am still with you (Psalm 139:1-18)!

Love,

I Am your Creator and Eternal Guide

POINTS TO CONSIDER

1. Father wants you to know that His thoughts towards you are very great.

2. Remember He knows everything about you.

3. There is nothing in your life that's hidden from Him.

4. He knows what you are going to do before you decide to do it.

5. He knows where you are going to be even before you know it.

6. He knows what you are going to say even before you say it.

7. He wants you to know that He is with you 24/7. He knows your secret thoughts and your hidden sins. You cannot hide from Him!!

BE ENCOURAGED TODAY MY LOVE

My love,

I want you to stand strong being reminded that My mighty power is at work within you!

I also want you to put on the full armor so that you can take your stand against the devil's schemes. Be reminded My love, that your struggle is not against flesh and blood, but against the rulers, against the authorities, against the powers of this dark world, and against the spiritual forces of evil in the heavenly realms. Therefore put on the full armor, so that when the day of evil comes, you may be able to stand your ground, and after you have done everything, you must continue to stand.

Stand firm then, with the belt of truth buckled around your waist, with the breastplate of righteousness in place, and with your feet fitted with the readiness that comes from the gospel of peace.

In addition to all this, take up the shield of faith, with which you can extinguish all the flaming arrows of the evil one. Take the helmet of salvation, and the sword of the Spirit, which is My written word. And pray in the Spirit on all occasions with all kinds of prayers and requests. With this in mind, be alert and always keep on praying for all the saints, everywhere.

Love,

I Am your Commander and Chief in Battle

POINTS TO CONSIDER

1. You must always be equipped for battle because you are in the battlefield of life.

2. When you submit your life completely to the Lord, He will equip you for battle.

3. In order to stand strong you must build a solid foundation for your life on God's word. You must read, believe, meditate and practice the word.

4. You must know the truth, God is truth, and His word is truth.

5. Remember your fight is not against flesh and blood but principalities, powers and evil and wicked spirits in the realm of darkness.

6. Exercise your faith as it is impossible to please the Lord without it.

7. Remember to use the Sword of the Spirit, which is the word of God in all your situations.

BE ENCOURAGED TODAY MY LOVE

My Love,

I will give you everlasting joy when you follow My instructions! You will be joyful when you obey My laws and search for Me with all of your heart, not compromise with evil and walk only in the path I have laid out for you.

My love, I have charged you to keep My commandments carefully, and reflect on My decrees, then you will not be ashamed when you compare your life with My commands. I want you to learn My righteous regulations and thank Me by living as you should.

My love, My precious daughter; I want you to follow My instructions and know that I will never give up on you.

I also want you to stay connected to Me because I Am the Vine Dresser, Jesus is the vine and you are the branch, so stay connected to Me and you will bear much fruit. (Psalm 27:10; 119:1-8& John 15:1)!

Love,

I Am your Joy and Integrity

POINTS TO CONSIDER

1. Father wants you to know that you will have great joy when you follow His instructions.

2. You will have great joy when you search for Him with all your heart, not compromise with evil, and walk in His ways.

3. Know that the Lord will never give up on you because you are His prized possession, you are His masterpiece.

4. Follow His instructions carefully and meditate in the word daily.

5. The word will teach you to be wise, so you can live a well disciplined life.

6. You will learn to reflect on the ways of the Lord.

7. And you will understand what it means to fear Him. To fear the Lord is the beginning of true wisdom.

BE ENCOURAGED TODAY MY LOVE

My love,

I want you to exercise your faith in Me, and when you asks, you must believe and not doubt, because those who doubts is like a wave of the sea, blown and tossed by the wind. They should not think they will receive anything from Me.

Have faith in Me. "I tell you the truth," if anyone says to the mountain, "Go, throw yourself into the sea," and does not doubt in their hearts but believes that what they say will happen, it will be done for them. Therefore I tell you, whatever you ask for in prayer, believe that you have received it, and it will be yours. And when you stand praying, if you hold anything against anyone, forgive them, so that your Father in heaven may forgive you your sins."

My love, never give up, ask and it will be given to you; seek and you will find; knock and the door will be opened to you. For everyone who asks receives; those who seeks finds; and to those who knocks, the door will be opened.

This is the confidence I want you to have in approaching Me; that if you ask anything according to My will, I hear you. And if you know that I heard you—whatever you ask for—you should know that you will have it!

(James 1:7 Mark 11:22-25Matthew 7:7-8 1 John 5:14-15)!

Love,

Have Faith in Me

POINTS TO CONSIDER

1. Father wants you to exercise strong faith in Him.

2. When you asks; you must believe and not doubt.

3. Know that without faith it is impossible to please Him.

4. Whatever you ask for in prayer, believe that you have received it, and it will be yours.

5. When you stand praying, if you hold anything against anyone, forgive them, so that your Father in heaven may forgive your sins also.

6. When you pray, never give up.

7. Continue to ask and it will be given to you; seek and you will find; knock and the door will be opened to you. For everyone who asks receives; those who seek finds; and to those who knocks, the door will be opened.

BE ENCOURAGED TODAY MY LOVE

My love,

I want you to know that when you offer up praise and worship with thanksgiving, and begin to cry out to Me for help this is what I will do for you.

I will part the heavens and came down to rescue you. I will shoot My arrows and scattered your enemies. I, My love, will expose them right before your very eyes.

I will reach down from on high and take hold of you, and draw you out of deep waters. I will rescue you from your powerful enemies, from your foes who are too strong for you, and when they confront you in the day of battle, I will be your support.

I will bring you out into a spacious place and rescue you because I delight in you; and I will deal with you according to your righteousness; according to the cleanness of your hands in My sight, I will reward you.

My love, when you keep My ways by turning away from evil, you will enjoy all the benefits I have promised you in My written word.

Be reminded that I Am not like men; or the sons of men who tell lies. I Am the Lord, your creator, and I will do what I have promised when you follow My instructions, so follow My instructions and reap the benefits (Psalm18:9-21&Isaiah 45:19)

Love,

My way is perfect

POINTS TO CONSIDER

1. Father wants you to know that there is victory and deliverance in your praise.

2. He will come down from heaven and rescue you from all your enemies.

3. He will be your support, and He will stand right besides you.

4. Know that He loves you, and He will cause you to be victorious.

5. Remember, He is a faithful promise keeper.

6. He does not tell lies like people do.

7. He is perfect, His ways are perfect.

BE ENCOURAGED TODAY MY LOVE

My love,

I want you to know that when you pray I will listen, I will bend down and listen to your prayers, so learn to practice forgiveness and I will forgive you of your sins when you have forgiven those who have sinned against you, and as you stay in covenant relationship with Me I will keep you from temptation and deliver you from the evil one.

My love, when you pray you must exercise your faith because without faith it is impossible to please Me; remember My love, you must be single minded about spiritual things because those who are double minded will not receive anything from Me.

My love, as you begin to humble yourself and pray; seek My face, and turn from your ways that displeases Me I will hear from heaven, forgive your sins, and heal your land. Then I will open My ears and eyes, and I will be attentive to every prayer when you cry out to Me, and though your sins are like crimson I will make them as white as snow.

My love, I want you to pray My word in every situation, because praying My word will make you as strong as a wild ox, and I will anoint you with the finest oil!

(Matt 6:12, 13; 2Chronicles 7:14&15; Isaiah 1:18; Psalm 17:6&92:10)!

Love,

I Am your Divine Intercessor

POINTS TO CONSIDER

1. Know that the Lord hears you when you pray.

2. Forgive those who trespass against you so you can receive forgiveness.

3. Father wants you live a life of humility.

4. Leave behind those things that are not pleasing to Him so your prayers will not be hindered.

5. Know that He is always ready, willing and able to forgive in an instant, as soon as you cry out to Him in repentance.

6. Remember to use the word in every situation as it is powerful, alive, sharp and active, and it always goes forth and accomplishes His purpose.

7. Praying the word will strengthen you spiritually because the word is spirit and life.

BE ENCOURAGED TODAY MY LOVE

My love,

My precious daughter, I want you to learn to serve others as I have served you, and since I, your Lord and teacher have washed your feet you aught to wash the feet of others, because I have given you an example to follow, so do as I have done for you. Now since you know these things, do them as this is the path that leads to your blessings.

My love, you need to know that even I, the Son of man came not to be served but to serve others and to give My life as a ransom for many, for all those who would believe and trust in Me.

My love, the apple of My eye, I want you to begin to pray for My will to be done in your life, not your will, but Mine be done.

My precious daughter! Know that you will become My friend when you learn to obey Me. Remember, My love, obedience is better than sacrifice and those who are willing and obedient will eat the good of the land, and things will go quite well for them.

(Matt 20:28; 26:39; John 13:14-15&17; John 15:15; Isaiah 1:19)!

Love,

I Am the One who teaches you love and obedience

POINTS TO CONSIDER

1. Imitate Jesus in everything you do and purpose in your heart to become a wise servant.

2. Purpose to do what you know is right, and receive the bountiful blessings.

3. Pray God's will be done in your life; and life's situations, as He knows what is best for you.

4. Know how precious you are to the Lord, don't allow the enemy to beat up on you, and know what Father says about you.

5. When you live in obedience to His word He will call you friend.

6. Things will go well for you.

7. Be reminded that the Holy Spirit is your teacher.

BE ENCOURAGED TODAY MY LOVE

My Love,

My precious daughter, I want you to know that I still rule from heaven and I watch everything closely, examining everyone in the earth, I examine both the righteous and the wicked and I will not tolerate anyone who loves violence. I will rain down blazing coals upon the wicked, those who love wickedness would be punished because I Am righteous and I love justice!

Righteousness and justice is the foundation of My throne. My unfailing love and faithfulness lasts forever and My faithfulness is as enduring as the heavens.

You need to know My love, that you and all those who do what is right will see My face, and happy are those who hear the joyful call to worship Me for they will walk in the light of My presence, they will rejoice always in My wonderful reputation and be exalted in My righteousness because I Am their glorious strength. Their power is based upon My favor.

My Love, I will not break My covenant with You nor change My mind regarding any of My promises made to you (Psalm 11:4-7& 89:2; 15-17 &34)!

Love,

I Am the One Who examines all motives

POINTS TO CONSIDER

1. Know that Father sits on the circles of the earth, He knows and sees all things, no one can hide from Him, even in the darkness at night He still see's everything, He knows what we are going to do or say even before we carry out the act.

2. He examines everyone and the wicked will not go unpunished.

3. Remember God is still holy and without holiness no one will see His face.

4. He rules with righteousness and justice because that's His character.

5. His love is everlasting, it's never ending.

6. You must worship Him in spirit and truth.

7. He will not break His covenant nor change His mind regarding any of His promises made to you!!

❤BE ENCOURAGED TODAY MY LOVE❤

❤❤❤

My love,

I want you to use My word in every situation, because My word is My voice.

You My love need to know that My voice echoes above the seas. It thunders over the mighty seas. My voice is powerful and majestic.

My love, My voice splits mighty cedars, it shatters the cedars of Lebanon, and makes Lebanon's mountains skip like a calf; My voice makes Mount Hermon leap like a young wild ox, and strikes with bolts of lightning.

My voice makes the barren wilderness quake and shakes the wilderness of Kadesh. My voice also twists mighty oaks and strips the forests bare, and in My temple everyone shouts, "Glory!"

Be reminded My love, I rule over the floodwaters, and reigns as king forever.

I give My people strength and bless them with peace.

My love, I want you to live holy, and honor Me for My glory and strength. Honor Me for the glory of My name, and worship Me in the splendor of holiness (Psalm 29)!

My love; be reminded to send forth My word in all of your situations so you can enjoy the benefits of the victorious life I have pre-ordained for you.

Love,

I Am your All Powerful Voice

POINTS TO CONSIDER

1. Know that God's word is His all powerful voice

2. His word is alive, powerful, sharp and active, and it goes forth and accomplishes His purposes.

3. It destroys principalities and powers, and evil and wicked spirits in the realm of darkness.

4. It splits mighty cedars and shatters the cedars of Lebanon.

5. It strikes with bolts of lightning.

6. It makes the barren wilderness quake.

7. His voice also twists mighty oaks and strips the forests bare, and in His temple everyone shouts, "Glory!" Use the word in all of your situations as it will destroy principalities and powers assigned to destroy your life.

BE ENCOURAGED TODAY MY LOVE

My love,

I want you to know that I will contend with those who contend with you, and fight those who fight you. I will take up My shield and buckler, and arise and come to your aid. I will come and help you because all of your help comes from Me.

My love, I will brandish spear and javelin against those who pursue you, and I will say to your soul that "I Am your salvation." Those who seek your life will be disgraced and put to shame; those who plot your ruin will be turned back in dismay, they will be like chaff before the wind, with My angels chasing them away.

My love, their path will become dark and slippery with My angels pursuing them and since they hid their net for you without cause, and without cause dug a pit for you, ruin will overtake them by surprise—the net they hid for you they themselves would be entangled; they will fall into the pit, to their own ruin.

My love, when you stay in covenant relationship with Me, by living holy and doing what you know is right, these are the benefits you will enjoy so you can live a life of peace and victory from the wicked (Psalm 35:1-8)!!

Love,

I Am a Shield round about you

POINTS TO CONSIDER

1. Don't be afraid of the wicked.

2. Know that the Lord has a protective shield round about you.

3. He will fight for you.

4. Remember Papa is your salvation.

5. Those who seek your life will be disgraced and put to shame.

6. The angel of the Lord will chase them away.

7. They themselves will fall into the pit they dug for you.

BE ENCOURAGED TODAY MY LOVE

My love,

I want you to know that I Am your refuge and strength. I Am always ready to help in your times of trouble, so do not be afraid when earthquakes come and the mountains crumble into the sea.

My love, I want you to know that because My spirit dwells within you the enemy cannot destroy you, know that I will protect you.

The nations are in chaos, and their kingdoms crumble, however, My voice thunders over the people, My word goes forth to accomplish My purpose and those who know Me are aware that My glorious presence are in the earth because they see My awesome works.

My love, I Am the One who brings destruction and causes wars to cease throughout the earth! I break the bow and snap the spear; I also burn the shields with fire. My love, the people of the nations need to be still, and know that I Am God. I will be honored by every nation, and I will be honored throughout the world because I live here among My people.

My love, I want you to know that I Am your fortress (Psalm 46).

Love,

I Am your Help in times of Trouble.

POINTS TO CONSIDER

1. Father wants you to know that He is your refuge and strength.

2. He is your very present help in times of trouble.

3. Know that He will not allow the enemy to destroy you.

4. The nations are in chaos; however, those who love the Lord will continue to stand secure.

5. His voice goes forth to accomplish His purpose.

6. He brings destruction and causes war to end.

7. The Lord will be honored among the nations, and every knee shall bow and every tongue will confess that Jesus Christ is Lord to the Glory of the Father!!

BE ENCOURAGED TODAY MY LOVE

My love,

Be reminded that I Am where your help comes from. Your help comes from Me the maker of heaven and the earth. I Am the one who created you and everything that was created; the birds of the air, the fishes in the sea, and the flowers of the fields, and I take care of them all. My Love, you are of more value to Me than they are, so just keep your trust in Me.

You also need to know My love; that those who put their trust in people are living under a curse because they do not trust Me, they have turned their hearts away from Me. Those who trust in people to meet their needs are like stunted shrubs in the desert with no hope for the future, but blessed are those who trust in Me, and have made Me their hope and confidence, they will become like trees planted along the riverbank with roots that reaches deep into the water, such trees are not bothered by the heat or worried by long months of drought, their leaves stay green and they go right on producing delicious fruit.

My love, I want you to know that the human heart is most deceitful and desperately wicked, no one knows it like I do, remember, I Am the One who searches all hearts and examine motives. You need to know that some will do things for you with the wrong motives, so I want you to be wise My daughter, and continue to seek first My kingdom and righteousness, and all of your needs would be met according to My riches in glory. Be thankful to those who do good things for you, thank them for their obedience to My voice to do the good deeds they have done, but know that the blessing comes from Me your Lord and King.

My love, My precious daughter; don't allow people to keep you in bondage because they have done some good deed for you. Use My divine wisdom My love, knowing that all your blessings comes from Me, your Lover and King

(Psalm 121:1; Jeremiah 17:5-10; Matt6:26, 27&33).

Love,

I Am your Provider, Discernment and Trusted Friend

POINTS TO CONSIDER

1. Father wants to remind you that He is your provider not people, and all the good things you receive; comes from Him.

2. Don't allow anyone to keep you in bondage because they have done a few good things for you. Remember, Father is your source. Be grateful and thankful to them for their kindness and their obedience to the voice of the Lord in helping you.

3. He will give you discernment when you are in covenant relationship with Him.

4. Continue to draw close to the Lord and He will draw closer to you.

5. Remember He calls you friend, and He will share things with you that He will not share with anyone else.

6. Purpose in your heart to build trust and confidence in God.

7. Know that the Lord is your Provider, Discernment and Trusted Friend, and He has everything you will ever need for a life of prosperity and success.

BE ENCOURAGED TODAY MY LOVE

My love,

I want you to begin your day by offering up praises to Me with thanksgiving; you also need to know My love that thanksgiving is a sacrifice that truly honors Me, so learn to glorify My Holy Name as you begin your day. This should be followed by praying the scriptures as they will give you hope and comfort for each day. They will teach you to keep asking, seeking and knocking until the door is opened to you.

My love, I want you to talk with Me about everything because I desire fellowship with you. Learn to pray My will be done in every situation you face as it is done is heaven knowing that My will is perfect.

Be reminded that the plans I have for you are all good and not for evil, and I Am always working all things together for your good, so pray My will, not your will, but My will be done.

My love, when you can't trace My hands; learn to trust My heart knowing that I want what is best for you.

(Matt 6:9, 10; Jeremiah 29:11; Psalm 119:49; 1Thess 5:17; Romans 8:28)

Love,

I Am your Divine Instructor

POINTS TO CONSIDER

1. Father wants you to become a worshiper, begin your days with praise, worship, adoration and thanksgiving.

2. He also wants you to pray the scriptures into your situations, because praying the scriptures will give you hope, comfort and peace.

3. They will also cause you to be persistent in your prayers.

4. Pray God's will be done in every situation because His will is perfect.

5. Know that His plans for you are always good and not for evil because you are very precious to Him, and He desires great things for your life.

6. Learn to trust Him in every area of your life.

7. Know that the Lord is your Divine Instructor.

BE ENCOURAGED TODAY MY LOVE

My love,

I want you to learn to follow My advice, and always treasure My commands. Obey My instructions and live! Guard them as you would your own eyes. Tie them on your fingers as a reminder and write them deep within your heart.

My love, listen to Me! For I have important things to tell you. Everything I say is right, for I speak the truth and detest every kind of deception.

My love, My advice is wholesome. There is nothing devious or crooked in it, and My words are plain to anyone with understanding, and clear to those with knowledge, so choose My instruction rather than silver, and knowledge rather than pure gold, for wisdom is far more valuable than rubies and nothing you desire can compare with it.

My love, I love all those who love Me, and those who search for Me with all their heart will surely find Me.

I have riches and honor as well as enduring wealth and justice. My gifts are better than gold, yes, even the purest gold, and My wages are better than sterling silver! I walk in righteousness, in paths of justice and those who love Me will inherit wealth, and I will fill their treasuries (Proverbs 7:1-3&8:6-11&17-21)!

Love,

I Am your Never Ending Wealth and Justice

POINTS TO CONSIDER

1. Father wants you to learn to follow His advice, and always treasure His commands.

2. Obey His instructions and live a well balanced and successful life.

3. Remember to write the word deep within your heart.

4. He wants you to know that everything He says is right, for He speak the truth and detest every kind of deception.

5. His advice is wholesome. There is nothing devious or crooked in it.

6. His words are plain to anyone with understanding, and clear to those with knowledge.

7. So choose His instruction rather than silver, and knowledge rather than pure gold, for wisdom is far more valuable than rubies and nothing you desire can be compared with it (Proverbs 7:1-3&8:6-11&17-21)!

BE ENCOURAGED TODAY MY LOVE

My love,

Do not worry about your everyday life, what you will eat or drink; or about your body, what you will wear. Is not life more important than food, and the body more important than clothes?

Look at the birds of the air; they do not sow or reap or store away in barns, and yet your heavenly Father feeds them. Are you not much more valuable than they? Can your worrying about things add a single hour to your life?

And why do you worry about clothes? See how the lilies of the field grow. They do not labor or spin. Yet I tell you that not even Solomon in all his splendor was dressed like one of these.

My love, If that is how I clothes the grass of the field, which is here today and tomorrow is thrown into the fire, will I not much more clothe you, O you of little faith? So do not worry, saying, 'What shall we eat?' or 'What shall we drink?' or 'What shall we wear?' For the pagans run after all these things, and your heavenly Father knows that you need them. But seek first My kingdom and righteousness, "Live Holy" and all these things will be given to you as well.

Therefore, do not worry about tomorrow, for tomorrow will worry about itself. Each day has enough trouble of its own (Matthew 6:25-34)

Love,

I Am your Divine Provider

POINTS TO CONSIDER

1. Don't worry about your everyday life—like clothing, food and the things the unsaved worry about; be concerned about what God wants you to do in each and every day.

2. Remember He takes care of everything He has created and you are more valuable to Him than they are.

3. Purpose to "Live Holy," seek first His kingdom and righteousness and all of your needs would be met.

4. Father wants you to trust Him with all of your heart and stop leaning on your own understanding.

5. Learn to cast all of your cares upon the Lord knowing that He truly is concerned about everything that concerns you.

6. He also wants you to know that He direct your steps and delights in every detail of your life; and He is working out the details for you.

7. Father wants you to know that He is your Divine Provider and He will continue to provide generously for you.

BE ENCOURAGED TODAY MY LOVE

My Love,

My love, if you will only obey My voice and allow Me to help you, things will work out wonderful for you, and as you begin to trust Me with all your heart and not lean on your own understanding, I, My love will order and direct your steps. So listen to My instructions, pay attention and grow wise. Seek first My kingdom and live holy and all your needs would be met according to My riches in glory through Christ Jesus. So I encourage you My love to begin to seek Me earnestly.

Be reminded My love, that the plans I have for you are good plans, plans to prosper and not to harm you. Know that I Am concerned about everything that concerns you and everything the enemy means for evil in your life, I will turn it around for your benefit and My glory; My love, I will give you beauty for ashes, so learn to commit all of your ways to Me and your plans will succeed.

You also need to be reminded that the purpose of My written word is to teach you wisdom and discipline, and to help you understand wise sayings. Listen to Me and treasure My instructions, tune your ear to wisdom, concentrate on understanding, and cry out for insight and understanding.

Love,

I Am your Creator who cares deeply for you

Proverbs 1:2, Isaiah 1:19; Proverbs 3:5&6; Proverbs 4:1;
Proverbs 2:1-3; Jeremiah 29:11, Isaiah 60:3; &Psalm 37:23&24

POINTS TO CONSIDER

1. God's word is to teach you wisdom and discipline and help you understand wise sayings.

2. Seek the Lord daily for wisdom, insight and understanding.

3. If you will put His word into practice for your life He will give you divine guidance and direction.

4. Seek first His kingdom and live a life of holiness.

5. Know that God has great plans for your life.

6. He is working out all the details in your life to bring you to rich fulfillment, to the place of safety and comfort you so long desire to be.

7. Learn to commit all of your ways to Him and your plans will succeed.

BE ENCOURAGED TODAY MY LOVE

My love,

When you pray, do not be like the hypocrites, for they love to pray standing in the synagogues and on the street corners to be seen by men. I tell you the truth; they have received their reward in full. But when you pray, go into your room, close the door and pray to your Father, who is unseen. Then your Father, who sees what is done in secret, will reward you. And when you pray, do not keep on babbling like the pagans do, for they think they will be heard because of their many words. Do not be like them, for your Father knows what you need before you ask Him.

This, then, is how you should pray: "Our Father in heaven, hallow be your name," your kingdom come, your will be done on earth as it is in heaven. Give us today our daily bread. Forgive us our debts, as we also have forgiven our debtors. And lead us not into temptation, but deliver us from the evil one.'

My love, if you forgive others when they have sinned against you, I will also forgive you, but if you do not forgive them of their sins, I will not forgive your sins either.

Love,

I Am your Teacher and Intercessor

POINTS TO CONSIDER

1. Father does not want you to become like the hypocrites, for they love to pray standing in the synagogues and on the street corners to be seen by others.

2. When you pray, go into your room, close the door and pray to your Father, who is unseen. Then your Father, who sees what is done in secret, will reward you.

3. And when you pray, do not keep on babbling like the pagans, for they think they will be heard because of their many words.

4. When you pray give honor to the name of the Lord.

5. Pray His will be done because His will is always best for you.

6. Ask Him for what you need for each day.

7. Forgive those who trespass against you so you can receive forgiveness.

BE ENCOURAGED TODAY MY LOVE

My love,

I want you to know that I delight greatly in you when you exercise everlasting kindness, justice and righteousness, and I will show My kindness to you by giving you rain from heaven and crops in season. I will provide you with plenty of goods and fill your heart with joy, so clothe yourself with kindness.

My love, be reminded that I show unfailing kindness to My anointed, for with everlasting kindness I will show compassion towards you. So I encourage you My love, to clothe yourself with kindness, and let My light shine brightly through you.

Love,

I Am your Everlasting Kindness

POINTS TO CONSIDER

1. Father wants you to know that He is well pleased with you when you exercise kindness, and help by bringing justice into unjust situations concerning others.

2. You will receive a bountiful harvest of blessings for your generosity and He will fill your heart with joy and gladness.

3. Let love be your highest goal in everything you do; allow the love of Jesus to flow freely through you.

4. The Lord will anoint you with the finest oil because you love what is good and hates what is evil.

5. He will use you in ways that He will not use anyone else because He can trust you.

6. Allow His light to shine through you always.

7. Remember to stay connected to Jesus, the true vine as He is the One who teaches you everlasting kindness.

♥*BE ENCOURAGED TODAY MY LOVE*♥
♥⚥♥

My love,

I want you to use wisdom, and think much about where you will spend eternity so you can make arrangements by living a life of holiness while you are still in the earth.

My love, the foolish woman only thinks about having a good time here and now, and as a result she chooses a life of destruction.

My precious one, you need to know that the road to eternity is narrow and only a few will find it, however if you will obey My teachings and build your life on the solid foundation of My word, by reading, meditating, believing and putting into practice all that you have learned, you will find the narrow road and stay on it.

I also want you to think about eternity while there is still time. Why perish for lack of knowledge, know that without holiness no one will see My face.

Be reminded that Jesus died for your sins, rose from the dead, and is right now sitting at My right hand making intercession for you, and all those who choose to live a life of holiness so you can all spend eternity with Me.

My love, give your body to Me, let it be a living and holy sacrifice, the kind I will accept; and think about what I have done for you by sending Jesus, My only Son to die for your sins; and the sins of the world.

(Romans12:1& John3:16; Eccl7:2&4; Hosea4:6; Hebrews12; 14; Matt7:13&14)!

Love,

I Am your Eternity

POINTS TO CONSIDER

1. Father wants you to live a life that is pleasing to Him.

2. He wants you to use the wisdom He offers that will help you make the right decisions for your life.

3. Know that the road to eternity is narrow, so purpose in your heart to find it and stay on the path.

4. Be reminded that it is only those who practice obedience will enjoy the bountiful benefits.

5. Offer your body as a living sacrifice to the Lord daily.

6. Learn to be thankful by counting all of your blessings.

7. Father wants you to think much about where you will spend eternity.

BE ENCOURAGED TODAY MY LOVE

My love,

Though the mountains may depart and the hills disappear, even then I will remain loyal to you. My covenant of blessing will never be broken!

I, your King rejoices over you, and I want you to know My love, that My love for you is better than wine. My left hand is under your head and My right hand embraces you!

My love, compared to other women, you My beloved is like a lily among thorns.

You are like the finest apple tree in an orchid, I have seated you in My delightful shade like fruit that's delicious to eat, and I will bring you to the banquet hall so everyone can see how much I love you.

I, My love, will feed you with My love while My left hand is under your head and My right hand embraces you (SOS 2:2,4&6; Isaiah 54:10)!

Love,

I Am your Romance

POINTS TO CONSIDER

1. Father wants you to know that He will always be loyal to you, and He will never break covenant with you, He will also show you off for all to see how precious you are to Him.

2. He rejoices over you with singing.

3. He carries you in His arms close to His heart.

4. You are blessed and highly favored, and you are very special to Him.

5. You are not just His lover but He also calls you friend because He can trust you, He will share things with you that He will not share with anyone else.

6. He will never let you out of His sight.

7. Know that nobody can love you like the Lord.

BE ENCOURAGED TODAY MY LOVE

My love,

I want you to become a vessel of honor to be used for My glory.

Are you willing to place yourself in My hands, being reminded that I Am the Potter and you are the clay? Are you going to allow Me to lead you like the shepherd leads the sheep so I can mold and make you into the vessel of honor that will bring glory and honor to My name? or do you just want to go through life leaning on your own understanding with little or no regard of who I Really Am, and the good plans I have for you? You need to think about this My love, the choice is yours; it's up to you!

My love, My precious daughter, My desire is to make you into a vessel that pleases Me. A vessel of honor! You need to know that "earthen vessels" are overlaid with silver dross, they have burning lips and a wicked heart, they are gossips, they talk too much, sows all kinds of discord and they are very, very lazy. They tell lies, the spirit of jealousy, anger, slander, immorality and all sorts of sins are operating in their lives, they are not wise at all and they lack self control!

My love, earthen vessels are very disrespectful to Me; they seem to forget that I am in heaven and they are in the earth and I can blow them away like dross anytime I have had enough of their complaining and criticism, anytime I so choose to.

My love, when you begin to fall in love with Me all over again, and allow the fruit of My Spirit to be evident in your life, you will become a golden vessel of honor, fit for the Master's use! You My love, must be sexually pure. There must not be any sexual immorality in your life! That means no adultery, fornication, homosexuality or any sexual sins because they displease Me. You also need to know that any sexual relations outside of the marriage covenant is sexual immorality, so present your body as a living sacrifice to Me, the kind I will accept.

You My love can become a vessel of Honor, one made of pure gold when you live according to My ways, so allow Me to mold you My love, into My image.

Love,

I Am your Potter

POINTS TO CONSIDER

1. Father wants you to become a vessel of honor for Him, to carry His glory throughout the nations.

2. Purpose in your heart to place yourself in the Potter's hand so He can mold and make you into the vessel of honor He would like you to become.

3. Are you willing to allow the Shepherd to lead you? Be reminded that the Shepherd leads the sheep, and when you allow Him to lead you, you will receive the benefits!

4. Father wants you to fall in love with Him all over again, remember He is your first love.

5. Allow the fruit of the spirit to be evident in your life as you learn to submit to His divine will.

6. Know that in order to become a vessel of honor fit for the Master's use there must be no habitual sins evident in your life, and you must have clean hands and a pure heart.

7. As you allow the Potter to mold you, you will become the vessel of honor, pure gold, which is the kind of vessels Father is looking for. Fit for His kingdom.

BE ENCOURAGED TODAY MY LOVE

My love,

My precious daughter, My desire is that you would purpose in your heart to praise Me at all times; I want you to continuously speak and boast only about Me, and My Son Jesus, and all I have done for you and your loved ones.

Tell everyone that I forgave your sins and redeemed your life from destruction, and I now shower you with radiance and joy.

My Love, I want you to learn to be confident that you will continue to see My goodness while you are here in the land of the living, learning to be brave and courageous, and as you continue to come and listen to Me, I will continue to teach you to fear Me, knowing that I Am your trusted friend.

My love, My precious one, I want your speech to be with grace and seasoned with salt at all times, because wise words come from the lips of people with understanding, so let your speech always be with grace because the wise is known for their understanding, and instruction is appreciated if well presented.

My love, you need to know that you are My masterpiece, created anew in Christ Jesus so learn to represent Me well!

(Col 3:17; Psalm 27:13; Psalm 34:1-3&11; Proverbs 10:13&16:21)!

Love,

I Am your Life's Designer

POINTS TO CONSIDER

1. Father wants you to become a worshiper.

2. Testify; tell others of all the great things He has done and continues to do for you and your loved ones.

3. Tell them that He redeemed your life from the pit, crowns you love and tender mercies, and fills you with radiance and joy.

4. He wants you to be brave, confident in His love for you, and courageous.

5. Seek first His kingdom and live holy.

6. Allow God's words to dwell richly in you, it will make you wise so you can be used as His mouthpiece.

7. He wants you to be known as His masterpiece.

BE ENCOURAGED TODAY MY LOVE

My love,

I want you to stand strong in all of My mighty power. Put on all of My armor so that you will be able to stand firm against all the devices of the devil.

I also want you to know My love; that your fight is not against flesh-and-blood enemies, but against evil rulers and authorities of the unseen world, against mighty powers in this dark world, and against evil spirits in the heavenly places. Therefore, put on every piece of My armor so you will be able to resist the enemy in the time of evil. Then after the battle you will still be standing firm.

My love, stand your ground, put on the belt of truth and the body's armor of My righteousness.

For shoes, put on the peace which comes from the Good News so that you will be fully prepared, and in addition to all of these, hold up the shield of faith to stop the fiery arrows of the devil.

Put on salvation as your helmet My love, and take the sword of the Spirit, which is My written word, and pray in the Spirit at all times and on every occasion.

My love, stay alert and be persistent in your prayers for all believers everywhere!

Love,

I Am your Spiritual Armor

POINTS TO CONSIDER

1. Father wants you stand strong being reminded that His mighty power is at work within you.

2. Put on the full armor so that you will be able to stand firm against all devices of the devil.

3. Know that your fight is not against flesh-and-blood enemies, but against evil rulers and authorities of the unseen world, against mighty powers in this dark world, and against evil spirits in heavenly places.

4. Put on every piece of God's armor so you will be able to resist the enemy in the time of evil. Then after the battle you will still be standing firm.

5. Know the truth and live holy, practice integrity.

6. Seek peace so you will be fully prepared.

7. Exercise faith to stop the fiery arrows of the devil and put on salvation as your helmet. Take the sword of the Spirit, which is the word of God, and pray in the Spirit at all times and on every occasion. Stay alert and be persistent in your prayers for all believers everywhere!

BE ENCOURAGED TODAY MY LOVE

My love,

Don't worry about the wicked and don't be envious of those who do wrong for like the grass they will soon wither, like green plants they will soon die away.

My love; My precious daughter, I want you to trust in Me and do good; dwell in the land and enjoy safe pasture. Take delight in Me and I will give you the desires of your heart. Commit your ways to Me, trust Me and I will do it.

I will make your righteousness shine like the dawn and the justice of your cause like the noonday sun. Be still in My presence and wait patiently for Me to act on your behalf, do not fret when people succeed in their evil ways, when they carry out their wicked schemes.

Refrain from anger and turn from wrath; do not fret—it leads only to evil.

Know that the wicked would be cut off, but those who hope in Me will inherit the land.

In a little while, and the wicked will be no more; though you look for them, they will not be found. But the meek will inherit the land and enjoy great peace.

My love; the wicked plot against the righteous and gnash their teeth at them; but I laughs at the wicked, for I know their day is coming. The wicked draw the sword and bend the bow to bring down the poor and needy, to slay those whose ways are upright, but their swords will pierce their own hearts, and their bows will be broken.

Be encouraged today My love, knowing that I will not allow the wicked to triumph over you. Bless them My love, don't curse them, remember vengeance is Mine, I repeat, vengeance is Mine, allow Me to handle your situations.

Love,

I Am your Shield from the wicked

POINTS TO CONSIDER

1. Take delight in the Lord and He will give you the desires of your heart.

2. You need to know that the Lord is your Shield and Protection, and He will protect you from the wicked.

3. Once you have learned to live in the secret place you will not need to worry about evil forces because you will have the benefits package of (Psalm 91).

4. Learn to wait on the Lord.

5. Don't operate in anger, don't allow anger to cause you to sin because angry people make wrong decisions, and remember; avoiding a fight is a mark of honor.

6. Know that the Lord laughs at the wicked and you need to do the same.

7. Be reminded that vengeance belongs to the Lord; He will repay your enemies!

BE ENCOURAGED TODAY MY LOVE

My love,

I want you to know that prayer is your key to victory. Please know My love that My word opens gates where only the righteous can enter with thanksgiving. It opens gates that lead to My presence and only the godly can enter there.

My love, I want you to put on salvation as your helmet and use the sword of the sprit which is My written word, you also need to know that your fight is not against flesh and blood enemies but against evil rulers and authorities in the unseen world, and against wicked spirits in the heavenly realm. My love, use every piece of My armor to resist your enemy, stand your ground, put on the sturdy belt of truth and the body's armor of My righteousness and pray at all times in the power of My Holy Spirit.

My love, you also need to know that praying My word will bring you hope and comfort. Don't give up, keep on asking and you will be given what you asked for, keep on seeking and you will find, and keep on knocking and the door will be opened to you.

Be reminded My love that you need to pray continuously, talk with Me throughout the day; came and talk with Me about everything being reminded that I desire fellowship with you.

My love, offer up praises with thanksgiving and honor My holy name. Glorify My name My love as you begin and end your day!!

Love,

I Am your Great Intercessor

POINTS TO CONSIDER

1. Father wants you to know that prayer is your key to all victory.

2. Your prayers will open gate that leads to His presence.

3. Use the sword of the spirit which is the word of God, because your fight is not against flesh and blood but against **principalities** and powers and evil and wicked spirits in the realm of darkness.

4. When you pray the word you will destroy Principalities and powers and evil and wicked spirits that are assigned against you and your loved ones.

5. Never give up, be persistent in your prayers.

6. Know that Father desires fellowship with you so purpose in your heart to fellowship with Him through prayer.

7. Remember you were made for worship.

♥ BE ENCOURAGED TODAY MY LOVE ♥

My Love,

My precious daughter, you need to know that I see your tears and feel your pain. Be reminded that I Am with you always, and I know and see all things that goes on in your life. Remember My love, that every day of your life is recorded in My book, and nothing in your life takes Me by surprise, so continue to trust Me, My darling, with all of your heart, soul, mind and strength. Do not lean on your own understanding. Remember the plans I have for you are good, and not for evil but to give you a future with great hope. Don't try to understand everything along the way, just trust Me!

My love, I also want you to know that I Am your refuge and strength, your very present help in times of trouble. My arms of love are always around you. I will never leave nor forsake you. I Am your comforter, Peace, Safety and Hope.

My love, I want you to continue to look to Me because I Am where all of your help comes from! Be reminded that I Am your (Lover ♥ ; Ephesians 1:4), (Husband; Isaiah 54:5) (Shepherd; Psalm 23), (Secret Place; Psalm 91:1), (Confidence; Psalm 27:13), (Promise Keeper; Isaiah 45:19), (Help; Psalm 121), (Trust; Psalm 125), (Intercessor; Isaiah 45:3-5), (Redeemer; Isaiah 54:5b), (Encourager; Daniel 10:19), and Restoration; and I will give you beauty for ashes (Isaiah 61:3)!

Be reminded My love that I Am your everything; so rest completely in Me as I accomplish My purpose for your life.

Learn to trust Me completely My love, knowing that I Am concerned about everything that concerns you; and I, My love, ♥ will send you help from My sanctuary and strengthen you from Zion (Psalm 20)!

Love,

I Am your Everything

POINTS TO CONSIDER

1. Father wants you to know that He sees your tears and feel your pain.

2. Remember that He is with you always.

3. He knows and sees everything that goes on in your life.

4. Remember that every day of your life is recorded in His book, and nothing in your life takes Him by surprise.

5. Trust Him with all of your heart, soul, mind and strength.

6. Remember that He is your refuge and strength, your very present help in times of trouble.

7. His arms of love are always around you. He will never leave nor forsake you. He is your Comforter, Peace, Safety and Hope.

BE ENCOURAGED TODAY MY LOVE

My love,

I want you to know that I Am not slack concerning My promises, and I did not make promises from some dark obscure place I didn't intend to keep.

You also need to know My love, My word says; eye has not seen nor ears heard, neither can the mind comprehend, the things I have prepared for those who love Me and are called according to My plan and purpose.

My Love, you need to know that I Am concerned about everything that concern you.

I delight in every detail of your life, and though you stumble sometimes you will never fall because I hold you by the hand, so learn to cast all of your cares upon Me, and I will sustain you because I never allow the righteous to fall.

Learn to trust Me with all your heart, soul, mind and strength. Do not lean on your own understanding, acknowledge Me in all your ways and I will direct your path.

You also need to know My love, that the plans I have for you are good plans, plans to prosper and not to harm you but to give you a wonderful future with great hope!

Know that all the ugly things that goes on in your life is not My plan for you, however, because of your love for Me, I will rescue and protect you because you trust in Me, and I, My love, will also give you beauty for ashes.

My love; My precious daughter, you also need to know that I lead with unfailing love and faithfulness all those who keep My covenant and obey My word!

My love; purpose in your heart to trust Me always; being reminded that I Am your Eternal Rock!

(Isaiah 45:19,1Corinthians 2:9,Psalm 25:10,37:23-24,91:14-16;1Peter5:7,Proverbs 3:5&6, Jeremiah 29:11).

Love,

I Am your Eternal Rock

POINTS TO CONSIDER

1. Father wants you to know He is a faithful promise keeper.

2. He's concerned about everything that concerns you, and He has great plans for your life.

3. Learn to cast all of your cares upon Him, and trust Him with all your heart.

4. Be reminded that He is your refuge and strength; your very present help in times of trouble.

5. He will lead you in the way you should go and guide you with His eyes.

6. He will also send you help from His sanctuary.

7. Know that He is your Eternal rock and He will give you strength to stand up against all evil forces.

BE ENCOURAGED TODAY MY LOVE

My Love,

Do not neglect to do good for those who need it when you have the opportunity to help them, if you can help them now, don't say come back tomorrow and then I will help you. My Love, be reminded that you are My Hands extended in the earth to meet the needs of My people, so do not forget to cast your bread upon the water, because after many days it will return to you.

Be reminded My love; My laws of sowing and reaping are at work in your life, so if you want good things for you and your loved one's; be good to those that comes to you for help!

Remember; My Love, My benefits for your generosity will be pressed down, shaken together and over flowing, you will not have room enough to contain it (Proverbs 3:27&28, Psalm 41:1-3)!

Love,

I Am your True Trust

POINTS TO CONSIDER

1. Whenever you have an opportunity to do something good for others just do it because you love the Lord, remember whatever you do should be motivated by your love for Him.

2. Be reminded that the laws of sowing and reaping are at work in your life, so you need to know that whatever you sow you will reap.

3. Remember that you are God's hands extended in the earth to get the job done, so look for opportunities to do the work of the Lord.

4. If you are stingy you will lose everything, purpose to become a generous giver especially to those in need.

5. Father wants you to know that you will receive manifold blessings when you take care of those in need.

6. You will begin to give freely when you have learned to surrender your will to the Lord.

7. Trust Him with all your heart, soul, mind and strength.

♥ BE ENCOURAGED TODAY MY LOVE ♥

My love,

I want you to know that My word, My instructions are wonderful; therefore you must obey them.

You also need to know My love, the unfolding of My words gives light, and it gives understanding to the simple. My word will cause you to open your mouth and pant like the deer by the water brook, longing for My instructions, and you My love will develop a strong desire to chase hard after Me.

My love, I will turn to you and have mercy as I always do for those who love Me; and I will direct your footsteps according to My word.

I will also redeem you from the oppression of people that you may obey My precepts, and I will make My face shine upon you as you continue to learn My decrees and follow My instructions.

Streams of tears will flow from your eyes and your soul will thirst for Me as the dear pants for the water brook.

My love, you will begin to realize that I alone, Am your Strength and Shield, it is to Me alone your spirit will yield, and I will become the number One desire of your heart.

(Psalm 41:1&119:129-136)

Love,

I Am all that you need

POINTS TO CONSIDER

1. Father wants you to know that His statutes and instructions are wonderful; therefore you must obey them.

2. Getting understanding in His word will bring enlightenment to you.

3. It will cause you to develop a great desire and longing for His instructions.

4. The Lord will have mercy on you as He always do for those who love Him.

5. He will direct your footsteps according to His word.

6. He will also redeem you from the oppression of people.

7. His face will shine upon you, and you will begin to realize that He alone is your strength and shield, and He alone is all that you need!!

BE ENCOURAGED TODAY MY LOVE

My love,

I want you to lead a life worthy of your calling, for you have been called by Me!

Always be humble and gentle. Be patient with others and make allowance for their faults because of your love for Me.

My love, I want you to make every effort to keep yourself united in the Spirit, binding yourself together in peace with others. For there is one body and one spirit, just as you have been called to one glorious hope for the future. Know that there is one Lord, one faith, one baptism, and one God and Father, who is over all, and is in all, and lives through all.

You also need to know My love, that I have given to each one a special gift through the generosity of Christ. That is why the Scriptures say, "when He ascended to the heights, He led a crowd of captives and gave gifts to them.

Notice that it says "He ascended." This clearly means that Christ also descended to our lowly world, and the same one who descended is the one who ascended higher than all the heavens, so that He might fill the entire universe with Himself.

Now these are the gifts Christ gave to the church: the apostles, the prophets, the evangelists, and the pastors and teachers. Their responsibility is to equip people to do the work and build up the church, the body of Christ, and this will continue until you all come to such unity in your faith and knowledge of My Son that you all may be mature in Him, measuring up to the full and complete standard of Him. Then you will no longer be immature like children. You won't be tossed and blown about by every wind of new teaching. You My love will not be influenced when people try to trick you with lies so clever they sound like the truth. Instead, you will speak the truth in love, growing in every way more and more like Christ who is the head of His body, the church. He makes the whole body fit together perfectly, and as each part does its own special work, it helps the other parts grow, so that the whole body is healthy and growing and full of love!

(Ephesians 4:1-16)

Love,

I Am your Healthy Spiritual Growth

POINTS TO CONSIDER

1. Father wants you to lead a life worthy of your calling, being aware of the fact that you have been called to be His hands extended in the earth.

2. Always be humble and gentle to all.

3. Learn to be patient with others, making allowance for their faults because of your love for Christ.

4. Make every effort to keep unity in the body of Christ.

5. Remember that there is one Lord, one faith, one baptism, and one God and Father who is over all, and is in all, and lives through all.

6. Be reminded God have given to each one a special gift through the generosity of Christ.

7. He wants to teach you to grow spiritually healthy so you will be well balanced in your spiritual walk with Him.

BE ENCOURAGED TODAY MY LOVE

My love,

You need to know that I Am a shield for you, the glory and the lifter of your head, when you cry out to Me I will hear and answer you, and deliver you from all of your Fears!

My love you need to be confident when you pray knowing that I pay attention to your groaning and listen to your cry for help, because I know that you will never pray to anyone else but Me.

I want you to know My love; that because of My unfailing love for you, you can enter My house with deepest awe and worship Me in spirit and truth. I will listen to your voice in the morning, each morning as you bring your request to Me and wait expectantly, I will answer you (PSALM 3:3, 4, 5:1, 2, 3, 7 &34:6)!

Love,

I Am the glory and the lifter of your head

POINTS TO CONSIDER

1. Father wants to remind you that He is a shield round about you.

2. He is your deliverer, and He will deliver you from all of your fears.

3. He hears your cries for help and answers, and He will send you help because He knows that you will not pray to anyone else but Him.

4. He wants to remind you to come boldly before His throne of grace and find help in times of need.

5. Continue to worship in the right attitude.

6. Learn to sit quietly and wait patiently for the Lord to act on your behalf.

7. Anticipate His inevitable, supernatural, intervention in your situations.

BE ENCOURAGED TODAY MY LOVE

My love,

Be truly glad, because there is wonderful joy ahead, even though you have to endure many trials for a little while. These trials will show that your faith is genuine. It is being tested as fire tests and purifies gold—though your faith is far more precious than mere gold. So when your faith remains strong through many trials, it will bring you much praise, glory and honor on the day when Jesus Christ is revealed to the whole world.

You My love have loved Him even though you have never seen Him. Though you do not see Him now, you trust Him; and you rejoice with a glorious, inexpressible joy.

You also need to know My love that your reward for trusting Him will be the salvation of your soul.

Love,

I Am your Inexpressible Joy

POINTS TO CONSIDER

1. Father wants you to rejoice, because there is wonderful joy ahead for you, even though you have to endure many trials for a while.

2. Know that your trials will show that your faith is genuine.

3. Your faith is far more precious than mere gold.

4. Continue to love Jesus even though you have never seen Him.

5. Thank Father God for loving you so much that He sent His only Son to die for your sins.

6. Rejoice with a glorious, inexpressible joy.

7. Remember your reward for trusting in the Lord will be the salvation of your soul.

BE ENCOURAGED TODAY MY LOVE

My love,

Make it your goal to live a quiet life, minding your own business and working with your hands just as I have instructed you in My written word, then people who are not Christians will respect the way you live, and you will not need to depend on others.

My love, I also want you to know what will happen to the believers who have died so you will not grieve like those without hope. For since you believe that Jesus died and was raised to life again, you should also believe that when Jesus returns, I will bring back with Him the believers who have died.

My love, those who are still living when Jesus returns will not meet Him ahead of those who have died. For He Himself will come down from heaven with a commanding shout, with the voice of the archangel, and with the trumpet call. First, the Christians who have died will rise from their graves. Then, together with them, those who are still alive and remain on the earth will be caught up in the clouds to meet with Him in the air. Then you will all be with Me forever.

So encourage yourself with these words My love (1 Thess 4:11-15)!

Love,

I Am your Encourager

POINTS TO CONSIDER

1. Make it your goal to live a quiet life.

2. Mind your own business and work with your hands just as Father has instructed you to do.

3. Father also wants you to know what will happen to the believers who have died so you will not grieve like those who have no hope.

4. Since you believe that Jesus died and was raised to life again, you should also believe that when Jesus returns, God will bring back with Him the believers who have died.

5. Those who are still living when Jesus returns will not meet Him ahead of those who have died.

6. Encourage yourself with the words of the Lord.

7. Oh, what a day of rejoicing that would be.

BE ENCOURAGED TODAY MY LOVE

My love,

Don't walk in the counsel of the wicked or stand in the way of sinners or sit in the seat of mockers, but delight in My laws and meditate in them day and night so you can become like a tree planted by streams of water which yields its fruit in season, whose leaves does not wither, and whatever you do will prosper.

I also want you to know My love; that is not so for the wicked, for they are like chaff that the wind blows away. Therefore the wicked will not stand in the judgment, or sinners in the assembly of the righteous.

My love, I watch over the way of the righteous, but the way of the wicked will perish.

Love,

I Am your Counsel

POINTS TO CONSIDER

1. Do not take ungodly counsel or associate with those who do wrong because bad company corrupt good habits.

2. Father wants you to take delight in Him by meditating in His word day and night, as it will help you to live a well balanced, disciplined and successful life.

3. Studying the word will also cause you to become like a fruitful tree that's planted by the riverbank, as the scriptures states; out of the abundance of the heart the mouth speaks, so as you hide the word in your heart you will begin to speak life and not death, your words will bring forth fruit.

4. Father wants you to know that the wicked has no future.

5. Pursue a life of holiness, as without holiness no one will see His face.

6. The Lord will watch over you continuously when you live holy.

7. Know that He is always available to give you counsel, He is always waiting for you to come and ask Him for direction.

BE ENCOURAGED TODAY MY LOVE

My Love,

If you listen to My instructions and faithfully obey them, I will keep My covenant of unfailing love with you as I promised with an oath to your ancestors. I will love you, and bless you, and I will give you many children.

I will give fertility to your land and your animals. When you arrive in the land I swore to give your ancestors, you will have large harvests of grain, new wine, and olive oil, and great herds of cattle, sheep, and goats, and you will be blessed above all the nations of the earth.

I, My love will protect you from all sickness and diseases. I will not let you suffer from terrible diseases, but I will inflict them on all your enemies.

My love, your children will be mighty in the land; your generation would be upright and blessed. Wealth and riches will be in your house, and your righteousness will endure forever. Even in darkness light will shine for you, for you will become gracious, compassionate and righteous.

My love, good things will come to you because you will become generous and give freely to those in need, you will lend freely, and conduct your affairs with justice.

(Deut 7: 12-16 & Psalm 112:2-5)

Love,

I Am your Covenant of Unfailing Love

POINTS TO CONSIDER

1. Father wants you to know that He will keep His covenant of unfailing love with you when you learn to practice obedience to His word.

2. He will cause you to become very rich and fertile.

3. He will protect you from all sickness. He will not let you suffer from terrible diseases, but He will inflict them on all your enemies.

4. Your children will be wise and successful.

5. Know that the Lord is with you always, even in difficult times.

6. You will be generous and give freely to those in need.

7. Know that the love of the Lord is unfailing, it is never ending.

BE ENCOURAGED TODAY MY LOVE

My Love,

You need to know that I hear your cries for help and I consider your sighing because I Am your King and God.

My love, I hear your prayers in the morning, every morning I hear your voice as you lay all of your requests before Me and wait in expectation, knowing that I Am not a God who takes pleasure in evil. I want you to know My love that the wicked cannot dwell with Me. The arrogant cannot stand in My presence, and I will destroy those who tell lies; bloodthirsty and deceitful men will not stand in My presence.

My love, I want you to come into My house; in reverence and bow down in My holy temple. I will lead you in My righteousness because of your enemies and I will make straight My ways before you.

My love, I want you to know that the wicked cannot be trusted, not a word from their mouth can be trusted; their hearts are filled with destruction. Their throat is an open grave; and with their tongue they speak deceit. I will declare them guilty; their intrigues will be their downfall and they will be punished for their many, many sins, because they have rebelled against Me and they refuse to come to Me in repentance.

My love, all those who take refuge in Me will be glad; they will sing for joy and I will spread My protection over them, and those who love My name will rejoice in Me, for surely I bless the righteous and I surround them with My favor as with a shield (Psalm 5)!

Love,

I Am your Shield and Favor

POINTS TO CONSIDER

1. Father wants you to know that He hears your cry for help.

2. Be reminded that He is your King and your God, He is concerned about everything that concerns you and He is working out all the details.

3. The Lord is your refuge and strength; He will send you help from His sanctuary.

4. He will lead you in righteousness because of your enemies.

5. Know that the wicked cannot be trusted, not a word from their mouth can be trusted.

6. Their hearts are filled with destruction. Their throat is an open grave; and with their tongue they speak deceit.

7. The Lord will surround you with favor as with a shield.

BE ENCOURAGED TODAY MY LOVE

My love,

Just as you accepted Christ Jesus as your Lord, you must continue to follow Him. Let your roots grow down into Him, and let your life be built on Him. Then your faith will grow strong in the truth you were taught, and you will overflow with thankfulness.

Don't let anyone capture you with empty philosophies and high-sounding nonsense that comes from human thinking and from the spiritual powers of this world, rather than from Christ. For in Christ lives all of My fullness in a human body, so you also are complete through your union with Christ, who is the head over every ruler and authority.

My love, When you came to Christ, you were "circumcised," but not by a physical procedure. Christ performed a spiritual circumcision—the cutting away of your sinful nature; for you were buried with Christ when you were baptized, and with Him you were raised to new life because you trusted in My mighty power which raised Him from the dead.

My love, you were dead because of your sins because your sinful nature was not yet cut away, I then made you alive with Christ, for He forgave all of your sins. He canceled the record of the charges against you and took it away by nailing it to the cross. In this way, He disarmed the spiritual rulers and authorities. He shamed them publicly by His victory over them on the cross, so don't let anyone condemn you for what you eat or drink, or for not celebrating certain holy days or new moon ceremonies or Sabbaths, for these rules are only shadows of the reality yet to come. And Christ Himself is that reality ((Colossians 2:6-17).

Love,

I Am your Mighty Power

POINTS TO CONSIDER

1. Since you accepted Christ Jesus as your Lord, you must continue to follow Him.

2. Listen to His teachings and build your life on the solid foundation of His word.

3. Don't allow anyone to capture you with empty philosophies and high-sounding nonsense that comes from human thinking and the spiritual powers of this world.

4. Be reminded that Christ is the head over every ruler and authority.

5. You also need to know that when you came to Christ He performed a spiritual circumcision—the cutting away of your sinful nature; for you were buried with Christ when you were baptized, and with Him you were raised to new life because you trusted in God's mighty power which raised Christ from the dead.

6. Know that He canceled the record of the charges against you, and took it away by nailing it to the cross.

7. Do not let anyone condemn you for what you eat or drink, or for not celebrating certain holy days or new moon ceremonies or Sabbaths.

BE ENCOURAGED TODAY MY LOVE

My love,

Don't let anyone condemn you by insisting on pious self-denial, or the worship of angels, saying they have had visions about these things. Their sinful minds have made them proud and they are not connected to Christ, who is the head of the body. For He holds the whole body together with its joints and ligaments, and it grows as I nourish it.

My love; be reminded that you died with Christ, and He has set you free from the spiritual powers of this world. So don't keep on following the rules of the world, such as: "Don't handle! Don't taste! Don't touch. Such rules are mere human teachings about things that deteriorate as we use them. These rules may seem wise because they require strong devotion, pious self-denial, and severe bodily discipline. But they provide no help in conquering a person's evil desires.

My love, I Am telling you this so no one will deceive you with well-crafted arguments.

I want you to know My love that I rejoice when you are living as you should and that your faith in Christ is strong (Colossians 2:4&18-23)

Love,

I Am your Rejoicing

POINTS TO CONSIDER

1. Don't let anyone condemn you by insisting on pious self-denial, or the worship of angels, saying they have had visions about these things. Their sinful minds have made them proud, and they are not connected to Christ at all.

2. Know that Christ has set you free from the spiritual powers of this world.

3. You also need to know that such rules are mere human teachings.

4. Know that manmade rules provides no help in conquering a person's evil desires.

5. Father wants you to know this so no one will deceive you with well-crafted arguments.

6. He rejoices when you are living as you should, and your faith in Christ is strong.

7. Remember, He whom the Son sets free is free indeed, and you have been set free to do the will of the Lord, so do not be entangled with human bondage!

❤*BE ENCOURAGED TODAY MY LOVE*❤

My Love,

I want you to know that I Am the Lord your God; and you must love Me with all your heart, all your soul, and all your strength. And you must commit yourself wholeheartedly to My commandments. Repeat them again and again to your children. Talk about them when you are at home and when you are on the road, when you are going to bed and when you are getting up, and write them on the tablets of your heart so you will not sin against Me.

My love, I will soon bring you into the land I swore to give you when I made a vow to your ancestors; Abraham, Isaac, and Jacob. It is a land with large, prosperous cities that you did not build. The houses will be richly stocked with goods you did not produce. You will draw water from cisterns you did not dig, and you will eat from vineyards and olive trees you did not plant.

My love, when you have eaten your fill in this land; be careful not to forget Me, who rescued you from slavery. You must love and respect Me and continue to serve Me, and when you take an oath, you must use only My name.

You must not worship any other gods, for I Am a jealous God. My anger will flare up against you if you do.

You My love must diligently obey My instructions—all the laws and decrees I have given you. Do what is right and good in My sight, so all will go well with you. Then you will enter and occupy the good land that I swore to give your ancestors. Your enemies would be defeated right before your face just as I said, and in the future your children will ask you, 'What is the meaning of these laws, decrees, and regulations that the LORD our God has commanded us to obey?' And you will say to them the LORD our God commanded us to obey all these decrees and to fear Him so He can continue to bless us, and preserve our lives as He has done to this day, for we will be counted as righteous when we obey all the commands the LORD our God has given us (Deut 6: 4-25).

Love,

I Am your Life's Preserver

POINTS TO CONSIDER

1. The Lord wants wholehearted commitment from you.

2. You must love Him with all your heart, soul, mind and strength.

3. Teach your children to love the Lord, obey and follow His instructions.

4. He will fulfill His promises He made to your ancestors, but He must first have your obedience in doing what He says.

5. As a result of your obedience to follow His instructions you will receive houses you didn't build, filled with all kinds of good things, and lands you didn't purchase. He will load you up with manifold benefits when you are obedient to Him.

6. Father wants to remind you not to forget all that He has done for you when you come into your blessings.

7. You need to know that He is a faithful promise keeper, and as you follow His instructions you will receive the benefits.

BE ENCOURAGED TODAY MY LOVE

My Love,

I want you to know that you are very precious to Me; so be encouraged, seek the peace that only I can give, do not be afraid of life situations and circumstances, be reminded My love that I did not give you a spirit of fear, but of power, love and a sound and well balanced mind. So stand strong knowing that you are very precious to Me.

My love, I want you to use the example of My servant David; though he faced many, many enemies, trials and tribulations; he encouraged himself using My word in all his situations as he spoke with Me continually.

Follow the instructions I gave to my servant Joshua; Do not let this book of the Law depart from your mouth; meditate in it day and night, so that you may be careful to do everything written in it. Then you will be prosperous and successful. My love, I also want you to know that all things will work out for your benefit because you love Me. I; My love, have called you for My purpose.

Be reminded that your help comes from Me, the Maker of heaven and earth. I will not allow you to stumble and fall because I watch over you. I do not slumber nor sleep!

I; My love watches over you—I Am your shade at your right hand; the sun will not harm you by day; or the moon by night. I will keep you from all harm—I will watch over your life; I will watch over your coming, and going both now and forevermore.

My love, I want you to come to that place in your life like My servant David where you can echo his words; that you are confident that you will see My good ness while you are here in the land of the living. My precious daughter, I also want you to know that you are fearfully and wonderfully made, My works are wonderful, know that I have created you in My image, after My likeness, and I watch over you as the apple of My eye, and as you walk in My ways you will become like a lily among thorns My darling while being confident and secured in My love for you!!

Love,

I Am your Encourager; Peace & Hope

POINTS TO CONSIDER

1. The Lord wants you to be confident and secure in His love for you.

2. His love for you is everlasting; it is eternal, never ending.

3. Know that He is working all things together for your good.

4. He wants you to build your life on the solid foundation of His word so you can stand strong when the storms of life come up against you.

5. Continue to look to the Lord being reminded that He is where all of your help comes from.

6. Be confident in knowing that you will see His goodness while you are here in the land of the living.

7. Always exercise strong faith as you wait patiently for His promises, His divine purposes to be fulfilled in your life.

BE ENCOURAGED TODAY MY LOVE

My love,

I want you to know that My Son Jesus return will come unexpectedly like a thief in the night when people are saying, "Everything is peaceful and secure," then disaster will fall on them as suddenly as a pregnant woman's labor pains begin. And there will be no escape.

But you My love aren't in the dark about these things, My dear, you won't be surprised when that day comes like a thief, for you are My precious daughter of the light and of the day; you don't belong to darkness and night, so be on your guard, do not sleep like others do. Stay alert and be clearheaded.

My love, night is the time when people sleep and drinkers get drunk, so live in the light and be clearheaded, protected by the armor of faith and love, and wearing as your helmet the confidence of your salvation.

I also want you to know My love; I chose to save you through My Son Jesus Christ, so you will know that He died for you, so that whether you are dead or alive when He returns, you can live with Him forever.

So I encourage you My love to build yourself up on My most holy word, and remember wisdom builds (1Thess 5:2-11)!

Love,

I Am your Wisdom Builder

POINTS TO CONSIDER

1. Father wants you to know that His son's return will come unexpectedly like a thief in the night when people are saying everything is peaceful and secure.

2. Remember you are not in the dark about these things.

3. You also need to remember that you do not belong to the darkness.

4. Be on guard; don't sleep like others do.

5. Stay alert and be clearheaded.

6. Wear as your helmet the confidence of your salvation.

7. Remember; Father chose to save you through His Son Jesus Christ, not to pour out His anger on you. Be reminded; Jesus died for you so that whether you are dead or alive when He returns, you can live with Him forever.

BE ENCOURAGED TODAY MY LOVE

My love,

I want you to stand strong, be at peace, be encouraged knowing that you are very precious to Me. Trust Me with all your heart and learn to cast all of your cares upon Me. My love, I will arise and set you in the place of honor where you so long desire to be.

Do not lean on your own understanding but acknowledge Me in all your ways and I will direct your path. I will bring an end to all unpleasant situations in your life, know that you are not going under but over in spite of all you sometimes see, hear or feel, and be reminded that I Am working all things together for your good and My glory.

My love, I go before you and make crooked places straight. I Am "The One" who brake bronze gates and cut through bars of iron to give you treasures hidden in darkness and riches in secret places and shows Myself strong on your behalf, so that you may know who I really Am!!

(Daniel 10:19; proverbs 3:5&6; 1Peter 5:7; Isaiah 45:3-5)!

Love,

I Am your Strength, Peace and Encouragement

POINTS TO CONSIDER

1. Father wants you to stand strong in His mighty power, don't be afraid of life's situations.

2. Know that you are very precious to Him.

3. Learn to trust Him, knowing that He cares deeply for you and He is concerned about everything that concerns you.

4. Stop leaning on our own understanding; trust Him with all your heart, soul, mind and strength.

5. Know that the Lord is working everything out for His glory and your benefit.

6. He goes before you and makes crooked places straight, and He defeats the enemy on your behalf.

7. Be reminded that He is your Strength, Peace and Encouragement.

BE ENCOURAGED TODAY MY LOVE

My Love,

I want you to know that I Am the One who forgives all your sins and heals your diseases. I Am the One who redeemed your life from the pit; crowns you with love and compassion, and satisfy your desires for good things, so that your youth is renewed like the Eagle's!

My love, I also work righteousness and justice for you when you are oppressed.

I have made known My ways to Moses, and I will do the same for you! You need to know that I am compassionate and gracious, slow to anger, and abounding in love. I will not always accuse, nor will I harbor anger against you.

My love, I don't even punish you as your sins deserve, or repay you according to your iniquities. For as high as the heavens are above the earth, so great is My love for you because you love Me.

As far as the east is from the west, so far I have removed your transgressions from you; as a father has compassion on his children, so I have compassion on you because you fear Me.

Be reminded My love, I Am the One who formed you and placed you in your mother's womb (Psalm 103:3-13; 139:13)!

Love,

Nobody can love you like Me!

POINTS TO CONSIDER

1. Father wants you to know that He is the one who forgives all of your sins,

2. heals your diseases, and redeemed your life from the pit. He crowns you with love and compassion; and satisfies your desire for good things so that your youth is renewed like the Eagle's.

3. He will bring justice in every unjust situation concerning your life.

4. He wants to show you His character as He builds character in you.

5. He has pity and compassion upon you. He does not even punish you according to your sins.

6. His love for you is everlasting that's the reason He calls you His prized possession (James 1:16).

7. Father wants you to know how precious you are to Him.

8. He wants you to know that His benefit package belongs to you because you are in covenant relationship with Him.

BE ENCOURAGED TODAY MY LOVE

My Love,

My precious daughter, you need to know that I see your tears and feel your pain. Be reminded that I Am with you always, and I know and see all things that concern you. Remember My love, that I Am your refuge and strength, your very present help in times of trouble.

I also want you to know My love; that the righteous has many afflictions, however, I deliver out of them all!

My love, I want you to continue to look to Me because I Am where your help comes from, remember I Am your Comfort, Peace, Strength, Way Maker, Redeemer and Strong Tower, so learn to rest in Me as I accomplish My will for your life.

Learn to trust Me completely My love, knowing that I will send you help from My sanctuary and strengthen you from Zion. Remember I Am the Glory and the lifter of your head, so arise and shine, and bring glory to My name (Psalm 34:19&46:1).

Love,

I Am your Comfort and Peace

POINTS TO CONSIDER

1. Father wants to remind you how precious you are to Him.

2. He sees your tears and hears your prayers, and He feels your pain.

3. He is with you always as He sees all things.

4. Be reminded that you will have many afflictions, but the Lord will deliver you out of them all.

5. Father wants you to continue to look to Him because He is where all of your help comes from.

6. He will send you all the help you need.

7. Know that the weapons may form, but they cannot prosper, they cannot prevail.

BE ENCOURAGED TODAY MY LOVE

My love,

Learn to shout for joy, be joyful at all times, and worship Me with gladness. Come before Me with joyful songs and worship at My feet.

My love, My precious daughter, you need to know that I Am your God.

I made you, and you belong to Me, you are Mine, you are My darling daughter the sheep of My pasture.

I want you to enter into My gates with thanksgiving, and into My courts with praises; be thankful always being reminded that thankfulness is a sacrifice that truly honors Me, so learn to praise My holy name always because I Am good. My love endures forever, and My faithfulness continues throughout all generations.

My love, be reminded that I have created you for My glory and not for yourself, so be willing to obey My instructions and you will enjoy the green pastures which is where your true happiness is found (Psalm 100).

Love,

Worship Me with gladness

POINTS TO CONSIDER

1. Father wants you to worship Him always.

2. Know that you were created for worship.

3. If you ever wondered what your purpose was, it is for worship.

4. Know that you belong to God, not yourself, as He has created you in His image, after His likeness so you can bring Him glory.

5. Learn to be obedient, follow His instructions as you read, believe, meditate in His word, and put into practice all you have learned.

6. Remember that there are manifold benefits for those who worship in spirit and truth.

7. Purpose in your heart to worship the Lord with gladness.

BE ENCOURAGED TODAY MY LOVE

My Love,

I want you to know that in times of trouble I will answer you, My great name will defend you and keep you safe from all harm, and I will respond to your cry!

Be reminded that I Am your shepherd, the One Who provide for all of your needs.

I Am your Green Pasture.

You also need to know My love, that I will keep you from being caught in all traps that the wicked would lay for you, because I Am your Holy Redeemer. I, My love will guide you with My counsel and lead you to a glorious destiny, because I Am your True Guide.

My love, those who trust in Me becomes as secure as Mount Zion, they will not be defeated but they will endure forever and ever, so I want you to learn to believe and trust in Me.

Pray in the Spirit at all times and on every occasion. Stay alert and be persistent in your prayers for all of My people everywhere. My love; learn to devote yourself to wholehearted prayer
(Psalm 20:1; 23:1; 73:24; 125:1; Proverbs 3:26; Ephesians 6:18)!

Love,

I Am The Answer to all of your prayers

POINTS TO CONSIDER

1. Father wants you to know that in your times of trouble He will answer you.

2. He will give you counsel, and lead you to your glorious destiny.

3. He will guide you in the way of wisdom and lead you along smooth paths for your life.

4. When you place your trust in Him you will become confident and secure in His love for you.

5. Pray in the spirit at all times and put Him in remembrance of His all powerful word.

6. Stay alert; don't be ignorant of the devil's devices, and devote yourself to wholehearted prayer.

7. Remember the Lord is the answer to all of your prayers.

BE ENCOURAGED TODAY MY LOVE

My Love,

I want you to know that when you stay in love covenant with Me, by living in obedience to My word, My mighty power will go to work within you. You also need to know My love; that I Am able to do far more than you could ever dare to ask or even dream of, infinitely beyond your highest prayers, desires, thoughts or hopes.

My love, My precious daughter, be reminded that the plans I have for you are all good, they are plans to prosper and not to harm you, they are to give you a wonderful future with great hope, so continue to come to Me with your ears wide open knowing that I Am concerned about everything that concerns you, I delight in every detail of your life, and I Am working out everything in your life for your benefit and My glory.

You also need to know My love; that I have created you for a specific purpose, to be used as a vessel of honor to carry My glory throughout the earth, so stay in the spirit My love, and you will not fulfill the lust of the flesh. Learn to listen for My voice so you can hear clearly when I say, this is the way, walk in it!

(1Corinthians 2:9; Jeremiah 29:11; Psalm 37:23&24; Psalm 119:105 & Romans 8:28)!

Love,

I Am your Lover and Spiritual Guide

POINTS TO CONSIDER

1. Father wants you to know that His mighty power will go to work within you when you stay close to Him.

2. He is well able to do way more than you can ever dare to ask or even dream of, infinitely beyond your highest prayers, desires, thoughts or hopes.

3. Remember He has good plans for your life, plans to prosper and not to harm you, but to give you a wonderful future with great hope.

4. He wants you to stay in constant communion with Him so you will know His voice, receive instructions and do what He tells you to do.

5. The Lord is concerned about everything that concerns you, and He is working it out.

6. You need to know that He is your Spiritual Guide, so allow Him to lead you by His Spirit.

BE ENCOURAGED TODAY MY LOVE

My Love,

You need to be reminded that the purpose of My written word is to teach you wisdom and discipline, and to help you understand wise sayings. Listen to Me and treasure My instructions, tune your ear to wisdom, concentrate on understanding, and cry out for insight and understanding.

My love, if you will only obey My voice and allow Me to help you, things will work out wonderful for you, and as you begin to trust Me with all your heart and not lean on your own understanding, I, My love will order and direct your steps. So listen to My instructions, pay attention and grow wise, seek first My kingdom and righteousness and all your needs would be met according to My riches in glory through Christ Jesus. So I encourage you My love to begin to seek Me earnestly.

Be reminded My love, that the plans I have for you are good plans, plans to prosper and not to harm you. Know that I Am concerned about all, everything that concerns you, and everything the enemy means for evil in your life, I will turn it around for your good, and My glory; I will give you beauty for ashes, so learn to commit all of your ways to Me and your plans will succeed.

(Proverbs 1:2, Isaiah 1:19; Proverbs 3:5&6; Proverbs 4:1)
(Proverbs 2:1-3; Jeremiah 29:11, Isaiah 60:3; &Psalm 37:23&24)

Love,

I Am your Creator Who cares deeply for you

POINTS TO CONSIDER

1. Father wants you to know that the purpose of His written word is to teach you wisdom and discipline and to help you understand wise sayings.

2. Listen to His voice and treasure His instructions.

3. He will show you great and might things which you know not of.

4. Purpose in your heart to seek first His kingdom and live a life of holiness.

5. Learn to pray His will, not yours in your life's situations.

6. Know that the enemy has no dominion over you.

7. Remember Father is your creator who cares deeply for you.

♥BE ENCOURAGED TODAY MY LOVE♥

♥❧♥

My love,

I want you to devote yourself to prayer so you can come to know Me more.

You need to know My love, that I have created you in My image, after My likeness and I delight in every detail of your life. You also need to know that My faithfulness towards you are very, very great, and I Am able to provide, heal, deliver, set free and restore everything that the locust and canker worm has eaten. Be reminded that I Am your Redeemer, so there's no need for you to live in fear.

My love; be reminded that I Am "The only One" who answers your prayers.

My word serves as a lamp to your feet that lights your pathway, so arise and shine for all to see My love, you need to know that I have set you apart and I will anoint you with fresh oil, and give you hinds feet so you can stand upon mountain heights without any fear of evil.

Be reminded My love, that I Am your Creator, Lover and Friend!!

Love,

I Am your Creator, Lover and Friend

POINTS TO CONSIDER

1. Father wants you to devote yourself to prayer because He wants you to know who He really is.

2. Know that you were created in His image, and you are very precious to Him.

3. He also wants you to know that His faithfulness towards you is very, very great, so there is no need for you to live in fear.

4. Know that He is the only one who can answer your prayers.

5. Study His word so you can make wise choices for your life.

6. He will give you a brand new anointing so you can stand strong regardless of situations in your life.

7. Remember that He is your Creator, Lover and Friend.

BE ENCOURAGED TODAY MY LOVE

My love,

I want you to devote yourself to prayer, learn to be watchful and thankful at all times.

Do not be anxious about anything, but in everything, by prayer and petition with thanksgiving, present your requests to Me. Be still in My presence My love, and wait patiently for Me to act on your behalf.

Be joyful always; pray continually; give thanks in all circumstances, for this is My will for you in Christ Jesus. And take the sword of the Spirit, which is My written word, and pray in the Spirit at all times and on every occasion.

Stay alert My love, and be persistent in your prayers for all believers everywhere.

(Colossians 4:2 Philippians 4:6; Psalm 37:71 Thessalonians 5:16-18Ephesians 6:17-18)

Love,

Give thanks in all circumstances

POINTS TO CONSIDER

1. Devote yourself to prayer.

2. Be watchful and thankful at all times.

3. Do not be anxious about anything.

4. Pray about everything.

5. Wait patiently for the Lord to act on your behalf.

6. Be joyful always.

7. Give thanks in all circumstances.

BE ENCOCURAGED TODAY MY LOVE

My love,

I will answer you when you call out to Me in prayer, and I will give you relief from your distresses; I will be merciful to you and hear and answer your prayers.

You need to know My love, that I have set you apart for Myself, because you were made for My glory, so I will hear when you call out to Me for help.

Offer the right sacrifices and trust Me My love; being reminded that I Am where all of your help comes from. I will fill your heart with great joy, and the light of My face will shine upon you.

My love, you will lie down and sleep in peace because I will cause you to dwell in safety (Psalm 4:1-8)!

Love,

My light shines upon you

POINTS TO CONSIDER

1. Father wants you to know that He hears you when you call, and He will answer your prayers.

2. You need to know that He has set you apart to be used for His glory.

3. Continue to offer up your sacrifices of praises with thanksgiving and put your trust in Him.

4. Know that He is where all of your help comes from.

5. He will fill your heart with great joy.

6. He will also protect you from all harm and cause you to dwell in safety.

7. Know that His light shines down upon you.

BE ENCOURAGED TODAY MY LOVE

My love,

I want you to know that the mountains may move and the hills may disappear, however, even then, My faithful love for you will remain, and My covenant of blessing will never be broken.

My love, you also need to know that My word is full of living power, it is sharper than the sharpest knife, and it cuts deep into the innermost thoughts and desires. I want you to pray My word, because My word is My will; and using My word will teach you to stay connected to the vine 'Jesus," being reminded that I Am the Vinedresser, Jesus is the vine and you are the branch!

Learn to repent often My love, and I will prepare in you a clean heart. You also need to know that continuous sin without repentance will hinder your prayers, so you must pray always so you will not fall into temptation, and when you pray, glorify My name, offer up praises with thanksgiving and remember My name is holy.

My love, when you pray don't keep on repeating the same words over and over again like the pagans do, for they think that they would be heard for their constant babbling, don't be like them.

Please know My love that I Am always with you. I see your tears and hear your cries for help. I will never leave nor forsake you, so learn to rest in Me as you practice My presence and anticipate great things!

(SR: Matt 6:7&9; 26:41; Lamentation 3:44 Psalm 51; John 15:1; Isaiah 54:10; Hebrews 4:12)!

Love,

I Am your Comforter and Hope

POINTS TO CONSIDER

1. Father wants to remind you that His love for you is eternal.

2. He will never break covenant with you as people sometimes do.

3. He wants you to hide His word in your heart so you will not sin against Him.

4. He also wants you to pray His word in all your situations as it will pull down principalities and powers, and spiritual wickedness in the realm of darkness.

5. Learn to repent often so there will be no hindrances to your prayers.

6. Know that God is with you always.

7. Be reminded that He is the one who gives you peace, comfort, encouragement and hope for each day.

BE ENCOURAGED TODAY MY LOVE

My love,

I want you to be happy. Rejoice, and honor "My Holy Name," for the time is close at hand, closer than it has ever been before for the wedding feast of the lamb, and you My love must prepare yourself, and when you have prepared yourself by practicing My presence daily, and keeping oil in your lamp, you My love will be permitted to wear the finest white linen.

Fine linen represents the good deeds you have done because you love Me, and have a great desire to see My kingdom come and My will prevail in the earth as it is in heaven, and because you continue to follow My instructions and live according to My ways; you have been blessed with great favor, and are invited to the wedding feast of the lamb.

Continue to worship Me, My beautiful bride as you continue to prepare yourself for My return (Rev 19:5, 7&9)!

Love,

I Am your Bridegroom and soon coming King

POINTS TO CONSIDER

1. Father wants to remind you to rejoice and be exceeding glad because the time is coming soon for the wedding feast of the lamb—the return of Jesus.

2. Anticipate the day of Jesus return to gather you and all those who belong to Him.

3. Prepare yourself for His return, keep oil in your lamp and wicks trimmed as you anticipate His return.

4. Continue to work on keeping your hands clean and your heart pure, because of your love for Him.

5. He will not forget all the good deeds you have done for His people.

6. Continue to pray His kingdom come, and His will be done in the earth as it is in heaven, being reminded that His will is always perfect.

7. Be reminded that Jesus is your bridegroom and soon coming King!

BE ENCOURAGED TODAY MY LOVE

My love,

I want you to burst into song, shout for joy, "enlarge" the place of your tent, stretch your tent curtains wide, do not hold back; lengthen your cords, and strengthen your stakes. For you will spread out too the right and to the left; your descendants will dispossess nations; and settle in their desolate cities.

Do not be afraid; you will not suffer shame. Do not fear disgrace; you will not be humiliated. You will forget the shame of your youth and remember no more the reproach of your widowhood.

My love, I Am your husband, the LORD Almighty is My name—the Holy One of Israel is your Redeemer. I Am called the God of all the earth. I will call you back as if you were a wife deserted and distressed in spirit—a wife who married young, only to be rejected," says your God.

My love, I will restore to you everything the locust and canker worm has eaten. I, My love; will give you beauty for ashes (Isaiah 54:1-6&63:1)!

Love,

I Am your Husband

POINTS TO CONSIDER

1. Father wants you to know that He will restore to you all the years that the locust and canker worm has eaten.

2. He will give you beauty for ashes.

3. He is your husband who cares deeply for you; He cares about your eternal soul, and His love for you is everlasting.

4. He will never break covenant with you.

5. He is the one who redeemed your life from the pit of destruction, crowns you with love and tender mercies, satisfies your desires for good things and renews your youth like the eagles.

6. He is your life planner and restoration.

7. He is your divine guide.

BE ENCOURAGED TODAY MY LOVE

My love,

Do not store up for yourselves treasures on earth, where moth and rust destroy, and where thieves break in and steal, but store up for yourself treasures in heaven, where moth and rust do not destroy, and where thieves cannot break in and steal.

For where your treasure is, there your heart will be also.

My love, the eye is the lamp of the body. If your eyes are good, your whole body will be full of light. But if your eyes are bad, your whole body will be full of darkness.

If then the light within you is darkness, how great is that darkness!

My love, no one can serve two masters. Either they will hate the one, and love the other, or they will be devoted to one and despise the other. My love, you cannot serve both God and Money (Matthew 6:19-24).

Love,

I Am your Treasure Chest

POINTS TO CONSIDER

1. Father wants you to stop chasing after, and hording things that moth and rust will on one day destroy.

2. Learn to be content with whatever you have because godliness with contentment is great gain.

3. Grasp a solid balance for your life.

4. Remember life has more value than the things you posses.

5. Where your treasure is there your heart will also be, and your life will be out of focus, your priorities will be out of order, and you will find yourself chasing after the wind, never having enough and always wanting more and more.

6. Remember, you cannot serve two masters, so choose whom you will serve.

7. Know that the Lord is your treasure chest; He has everything you will ever need in this life and the one to come, so seek first His kingdom and live holy.

BE ENCOURAGED TODAY MY LOVE

My love,

Be reminded that I Am a shield around you, and I Am the glory and the lifter up of your head.

My love, I know that you have many, many foes; however, you must remember that I sit in the heavens from where I see everything that go on in your life! There are many who rise up against you; they say I will not deliver you because they don't really know who I Am. I want you to know that I will arise and deliver you from your enemies. I will strike all of them on the jaw and they will be defeated right before your face.

You My love, will not be afraid of tens of thousands who comes up against you on every side, because you will be confident in My love for you, knowing that your deliverance comes from Me, and My blessings is upon you.

You My love, will be able to lie down and sleep in safety knowing that I Am the One Who sustains you and keep you safe from the wicked (Psalm 3: 1-8)!

Love,

I Am your Shield from the wicked

POINTS TO CONSIDER

1. Father wants you to know that He shields you from the wicked.

2. He's quite aware that you have many, many foes.

3. Remember He sits over the nations and He sees everything.

4. You need to know that He fights for you and will continue to do so.

5. When the enemy comes in before you in one way, they will flee in seven.

6. You will not need to live in fear.

7. The Lord will rescue you because you love Him, and protect you because you trust in His name.

BE ENCOURAGED TODAY MY LOVE

My love,

I want you to learn to exercise self control; that means to show control or restraint for your life, because a woman who lacks self control is like a city broken down without walls. You also need to know My love, that there is no law against self control.

My love, My precious daughter; don't be like those who are in darkness. I want you to live in the light, and since you belong to the light, learn to exercise self control. Put on faith and love as a breast plate, and the hope of salvation as a helmet. My love, I want you to know that those who lack self control are without love, unforgiving, slanderous; brutal and hate what is good.

On the other hand a self controlled woman is pure; and busy with the things of the Lord and her family; she is kind, loving, and compassionate. The fruit of the spirit is evident in her life. She is loving, joyful, patient, peaceful; kind and gentle, and exercises self control. Her family rises up and calls her blessed. She has learned to say no to ungodliness and worldly passions, and endeavors to live a self controlled, upright and godly life.

My love, I want you to prepare you mind for action and set your heart on the grace to be given to you when Jesus is revealed, be clear minded and self controlled so that you can pray.

Be reminded My love, that a woman who fears the Lord she shall be greatly praised, and I will make her My masterpiece.

So I encourage you to build your spacious house My daughter; and hewn out your seven pillars as you allow My gentle spirit to lead you in the way you should go and guide you with My eyes.

(Proverbs 25:8; 31:10:28&30; Gal 5:23; 1Thess 5:6&8; 2Tim3:3; Titus 1:8; Titus2:12; 1Peter1:13; 1Peter4:7)!

Love,

I Am your Fruit in the Spirit

POINTS TO CONSIDER

1. Father wants you to exercise self control, as those who exercise self control carries a mark of honor.

2. The woman who lacks self control is like a city broken down without walls.

3. Since you belong to the light, you must walk in the light; that means you must put away your old ways and leave behind those things that are not pleasing to the Lord!!

4. Know that people who lack self control get into all kinds of trouble, and the Lord is not pleased with them.

5. A woman who exercises self control is busy with her family and the things of the Lord, she is not found with idle company. She is clear minded so she can receive instructions from the Lord to pray for family, others and self.

6. She allows Father's gently spirit to lead her.

7. She makes love her highest calling, and the fruit of the spirit are at work in her life.

BE ENCOURAGED TODAY MY LOVE

My love,

My love, I Am your Redeemer; the Holy One of Israel, your Creator and King.

I made the way through the sea, a path through the mighty waters.

Be reminded that I have created you. I knitted you together and placed you in your mother's womb. 'There is no need for you to live in fear." Fear not, for I have redeemed you. I have summoned you by name; you are Mines. When you pass through the waters, I will be with you; and when you pass through the rivers, they will not sweep over you. When you walk through the fire, you will not be burned; the flames will not set you ablaze. For I Am the LORD, your God, the Holy One of Israel, your Savior. You need to know My love; that you are precious and honored in My sight, because I love you.

Do not be afraid, for I Am always with you; I will bring your children from the east and gather you from the west, and I will say to the north, 'Give them up,' and to the south, 'Do not hold them back.' I will bring your sons from afar and your daughters from the ends of the earth!

My love, be reminded that I Am the One who drew out the chariots and horses, the army and reinforcements together, and they lay there, never to rise again, extinguished, and snuffed out like a wick.

My love; "Forget the former things; and do not dwell on the past.

Love,

I Am your Eternal Destiny

(Isaiah 43:1-7 & 14-18)

POINTS TO CONSIDER

1. Father wants you to know that you are highly favored and He is with you always.

2. Do not be afraid of life's situations.

3. He will bring the rebellious children back to Him.

4. Be reminded that nothing is impossible when you place your trust in God.

5. He will continue to make ways for you where there seems to be no way.

6. Forget about your past and move forward to your glorious destiny in Christ Jesus.

7. Remember; Father holds your eternal destiny.

♥BE ENCOURAGED TODAY MY LOVE♥

My love,

The nations are in rebellion and the people plot in vain. The leaders take their stand, and the rulers gather together against Me, and My anointed ones, they say; let us break their chains, and throw off their fetters, make a mockery of what they do, and believe in, however I sit in the heavens and laugh, I scoff at them.

I will rebuke them My love. My precious one, be wise and serve Me with reverent fear, being reminded that walking in obedience to My word is the beginning of true wisdom. Remember My love that the wisdom of the world is foolishness to Me, so learn to seek My wisdom so you can enjoy the life of prosperity and success which I had promised to your ancestors long ago!

My love; tune your ears to wisdom, and concentrate on understanding. Cry out for insight, and ask for understanding. Search for them as you would for silver; seek them like hidden treasures, then you will understand what it means to fear Me, and you will gain knowledge of Who I really Am.

My love, I grant wisdom, and from My mouth comes knowledge and understanding.

I grant a treasure of common sense to the honest, and I serve as a Shield to those who walk with integrity. I also guard the paths of the just and protect those who are faithful to Me (Psalm 2:1-11&Proverbs 2:3-8).

Love,

I Am your Spiritual Guide

POINTS TO CONSIDER

1. Father wants you to know that people are in rebellion against Him and they plan all kinds of wickedness which will never prevail.

2. The leaders are also in rebellion, they scoff at the ways of the Lord.

3. They make fun of Christians, those anointed of the Lord.

4. The Lord laughs at the wicked for He knows what their end will be.

5. Be wise, keep your eyes upon the Lord and stay focused.

6. Be reminded that the Lord is all wisdom; remember the wisdom of the world is foolishness to Him.

7. Tune your ears to wisdom and concentrate on understanding, cry out for insight and Father will guide you into all truth.

BE ENCOURAGED TODAY MY LOVE

My love,

Be reminded that My word is a lamp to guide your feet, and a light for your path, and I want you to obey My righteous regulations.

My love, I know that you have suffered much, but I will restore your life again just as I have promised. I will accept your offerings of praise, and teach you My regulations, and as you continuously obey My instructions your life will not hang in the balance.

Be reminded My love that the wicked are always setting traps for you, however, as you learn to trust Me and treasure My instructions, make them your hearts delight, and determine to keep My ways throughout the very end, I will continuously fight for you and silence your enemies (Psalm 119: 105-112)!

Love,

I Am your Spiritual Balance

POINTS TO CONSIDER

1. Know that the Lord orders and directs your steps.

2. Obey His word so you can live a well balanced life.

3. Remember the wicked are always setting traps for you; however no weapon formed against you shall prosper.

4. The wicked will be caught in their own traps.

5. The pit they dig for you, they will fall into it.

6. The gallows they build for you they will be hung on it.

7. Know that your fight is not against flesh and blood people, but wicked spirits in the realm of darkness, so use the sword of the spirit which is the word of the Lord in all of your situations.

BE ENCOURAGED TODAY MY LOVE

My love,

I want you to press on to possess the perfection for which Christ Jesus first possessed you.

Focus on this one thing: Forget the past and look forward to what lies ahead of you. Press on to reach the end of the race and receive the heavenly prize for which I, through Christ Jesus, am calling you.

My love, desire spiritual maturity so you can embrace the holy things, and you must hold on to the progress you have already made.

My love, I also want you to pattern your life after Mine, and learn from those who follow My example, for I have told you often before, and I say it again, My spirit are grieved because there are many whose conduct shows they are really enemies of the cross of Christ; they are headed for destruction. Their god is their appetite, they brag about shameful things, and they think only about this life here on earth.

My love, they criticize heaven, where the Lord Jesus Christ lives. You My love, should eagerly wait for His return. He will take your weak mortal body and change it into a glorious body like His own, using the same power with which He will bring everything under His control (Philippians 3:12-17)!

Love,

I Am your Perfection in Christ

POINTS TO CONSIDER

1. Father wants you to purpose in your heart to live a life of holiness.

2. Forget the past and look forward to what lies ahead of you.

3. Desire spiritual maturity so you can embrace the holy things of God.

4. You must hold on to the progress you have already made, and continue to move forward.

5. Do not bring grief to the Holy Spirit as the heathens do.

6. Anticipate the return of Jesus who will make all things perfect.

7. He will take your weak body and make it into a glorious one.

BE ENCOURAGED TODAY MY LOVE

My love,

Live no longer as the heathens do, for they are hopelessly confused. Their minds are full of darkness; they wander far from the life I give because they have closed their minds and hardened their hearts against Me! They have no sense of shame. They live for lustful pleasure and eagerly practice every kind of impurity. But that isn't what you learned about Christ since you have heard about Jesus and have learned the truth that comes from Him.

My love, I want you to throw off your old sinful nature and your former way of life, which is corrupted by lust and deception. Instead, let My Spirit renew your thoughts and attitudes. Put on your new nature created to be like Jesus—truly righteous and holy. So stop telling lies, tell your neighbors the truth, for you are all parts of the same body, and "don't sin by letting anger control you, and certainly don't let the sun go down while you are still angry for anger gives a foothold to the devil.

My love, if you are a thief, quit stealing. Instead, use your hands for good hard work, and then give generously to others in need. Don't use foul or abusive language. Let everything you say be good and helpful so that your words will be an encouragement to those who hear them, and do not bring sorrow to My Holy Spirit by the way you live. Remember, I have identified you as My own, guaranteeing that you will be saved on the day of redemption.

My love, My precious daughter get rid of all bitterness, rage, anger, harsh words, and slander, as well as all types of evil behavior. Instead; be kind to others, tenderhearted, and forgiving others, just as I, through Christ have forgiven you (Ephesians 4:17-32).

Love,

I Am your Guaranteed Redemption

POINTS TO CONSIDER

1. Father is saying; live no longer as the heathens do, for they are hopelessly confused.

2. He wants you to throw off your old sinful nature and your former way of life, which is corrupted by lust and deception. Instead, let His Spirit renew your thoughts.

3. You should be different in the way you think and behave.

4. If you are a thief, quit stealing. Instead, use your hands for good hard work, and then give generously to those in need.

5. Don't use foul or abusive language. Let everything you say be good and helpful, so that your words will be an encouragement to those who hear them.

6. Pray that the Lord will prepare in you a clean heart and renew your thoughts and attitude. Don't allow anger to have a foothold over you.

7. Put on your new nature, created to be like Jesus—truly righteous and holy.

BE ENCOURAGED TODAY MY LOVE

My love,

Don't be selfish, and don't try to impress others. Practice humility, and think the best of other people. Don't look out only for your own interests, but take an interest in others also.

My love, you must have the same attitude that Christ Jesus had though He was God, He did not think of equality with Me as something to cling to. Instead, He gave up His divine privileges and took the humble position of a slave, and was born as a human being.

My love, when He appeared in human form, He humbled Himself in obedience to Me and died a criminal's death on a cross. Therefore, I elevated Him to the place of highest honor, and gave Him the name above all other names, that at the sound of His name "Jesus" every knee shall bow, in heaven and earth, and under the earth, and every tongue shall confess that Jesus Christ is Lord, all to glorify My holy name (Philippians 2:3-11).

Love,

I Am your Glory

POINTS TO CONSIDER

1. Don't be selfish; don't look out only for your own interests, but take an interest in others also.

2. Practice humility, and don't try to impress people.

3. You must have the same attitude Jesus Christ had even though He was God.

4. Learn to humble yourself, and practice obedience.

5. Look for opportunities to be a blessing to others.

6. Give glory to God.

7. Be reminded that the Lord made you for His glory and not for yourself.

BE ENCOURAGED TODAY MY LOVE

My love,

I want you to know that you are very precious to Me. You, My love are very, very special, that's the reason I refer to you as the apple of My eye. You also need to know that you are fearfully and wonderfully made, and you are marvelous in My sight.

You are My prized possession, and I love you more than anything I have created throughout the entire universe. My love, My darling daughter, My princess, you need to be reminded that I, your King, have created you in My image, after My likeness and have equipped you with everything you will ever need to live as the beautiful princess I have created you to be. Know who you are My darling, because you are royalty.

My love, My banner over you is love, so please don't settle for any less than what I had purposed for you in My divine plan at creation. Be reminded My love, the plans I have for you are good plans, plans to prosper and not to harm you, but to give you a wonderful future as you continue to live up to the calling I have placed upon your life. Remember My love, My darling princess, all I require from you as you fulfill the role of princess is obedience to My written word, and purpose in your heart to love Me with all your heart, soul, mind and strength, while making Me priority number one in your life!!

My love, as you begin to practice My presence by beginning and ending your day with praise, worship, adoration and prayer, you will begin to draw close to Me, and as a result I will draw closer to you, then you will begin to understand who I really Am, and who I have created you to be.

You My love, will begin to understand why I call you; designer's original, apple, lily, and prized possession. You My love must learn to stand confident in My great love for you.

(Daniel 10:19; Psalm 17:8; Genesis 1:26-28; Jeremiah 29:11; Isaiah 1:19;139:14)

Love,

You are My prize possession

POINTS TO CONSIDER

1. Father wants you to know that you are very, very precious to Him.

2. Remember He created you in His image, after His likeness and calls you His masterpiece.

3. He also wants you to know that He has already equipped you with everything you will ever need to live the abundant life He has in store for you.

4. Learn to tap into the source by drawing closer to Him, He will show you His character. His character is holiness.

5. Practice His presence daily, talk with Him about everything.

6. Begin your day with Praise, worship, adoration and prayer.

7. You will begin to understand why He calls you; designer's original, apple, lily, and prize possession.

BE ENCOURAGED TODAY MY LOVE

My love,

My precious daughter, I want you to learn to seek peace, turn away from evil and do good, and work hard at living at peace with others.

My love, as you draw close to Me, I will draw closer to you, so build your life upon the solid foundation of My written word by meditating in the bible day and night for a life of prosperity and success, and as a result you will be connected to the true vine Who is My Son Jesus, so when the storms of life comes up against you, you will remain standing strong. My love, you also need to pray continuously. I want you to talk with Me about everything.

My precious daughter I want you to become like Mary, the sister of Martha who had her priorities in order and chose to listen to Jesus instead of worrying about things that has no lasting value, things that moth and rust will destroy one day, things that the fire will burn up on the day of My Son's return, so set your priorities in order putting Me first in everything you do, knowing that without Me you can do nothing of value that will in turn prepare you for eternity. My love; be still and know that I Am God, know that I rule in the affairs of your life!

Don't worry about anything My love, but pray about everything, tell Me what you need, and thank Me for all I have done, if you do this you will experience My perfect peace which is far more wonderful than the human mind can understand.

My love, My precious daughter; allow My peace to guard Your heart and mind as you live in Christ Jesus!

(Psalm 34:14; 46:10; Matt 7:24&25; Joshua 1:8; John 15:1; 1Thess 5:17; Luke 10:38-42; Philipp: 4:6&7)!

Love,

I Am your Perfect Peace

POINTS TO CONSIDER

1. The Lord wants you to learn to seek peace and pursue it.

2. Purpose in your heart to build your life on the solid foundation of His word.

3. Meditate in the word day and night and allow the word to dwell richly in you as it will cause you to become a person of great wisdom and understanding.

4. Make the Lord your priority, set aside quality time to spend with Him.

5. Pray always, talk to Him about everything.

6. Know that He is God. He is in control of your life.

7. Allow Him to lead you into green pastures beside still waters, being reminded that He is the only one who can restore your soul.

BE ENCOURAGED TODAY MY LOVE

My love,

I want you to learn to love My instructions, and think about them all day long; and follow through by doing what it says. My commandments will make you wiser than your enemies. They will guide you continuously and give you insight for living a life of holiness.

My love, I want you to purpose in your heart to study My word daily so you will learn to keep My ways by following My instructions. Learn to choose the good and refuse to walk on any evil path so that you may remain obedient to My word.

My love, don't turn away from My regulations, for I have taught you well. You also need to know My love, My words are sweet; they are sweeter than honey. They will give you understanding and you will learn to hate every false way.

You My love will be able to discern the difference between good and evil and I will bless you for your obedience (Psalm 119:97-104)!

Love,

I Am your Insight for Living

POINTS TO CONSIDER

1. Father wants you to practice obedience by following His instructions.

2. He wants you to read and meditate in His word, and think about what He is saying to you, and they will guide you continually, and give you insight for life.

3. The word will equip you to live a disciplined and well balanced life.

4. Develop a desire for His word more than anything else this world has to offer.

5. They will give you a sense of discernment to discern between right and wrong.

6. They word will help you make wise decisions regarding your life.

7. They will keep you heart softened, and keep you in a right relationship with the Lord.

BE ENCOURAGED TODAY MY LOVE

My love,

I want you to know that because of My unfailing love for you, and your obedience to My written word, when you are in distress I will protect you. I will send you help from My sanctuary and grant you support from Zion. I will remember all your sacrifices, offerings and gifts to the poor and needy.

My love, I will give you the desires of your heart and make all your plans succeed.

Others will shout for joy with you when you are victorious, they will rejoice with you in My name, and I will grant you all of your requests and desires of your heart so you will know that I have kept all of My promises made to you!

My love, some trust in chariots and horses "Their wealth and riches" but I want you to trust Me. Those who trust in their wealth and riches will be brought to their knees and fall, but you will rise and stand firm when you have learned to trust in Me the maker of heaven and earth Who created everything (Psalm 20)!

Love,

I Am your Help

POINTS TO CONSIDER

1. Father wants you to know that He is always with you in your times of trouble.

2. He will make ways for you where there seem to be no other way.

3. He will give you the desires of your heart and all of your plans will succeed when you learn to trust Him.

4. Those of like mind will rejoice with you.

5. He will bless you because you have trusted in Him and not the things you possessed.

6. Be reminded that He is the one who created you and everything that was ever created, and you are very important to Him.

7. Know that the Lord is where all of your help comes from.

BE ENCOURAGED TODAY MY LOVE

My love,

When you do what is right and just I will not leave you to your oppressors. I will ensure your well-being so the arrogant will not oppress you.

My love, I will deal with you according to My great love for you, and I will teach you My ways because you are My servant. I, My love will give you discernment that you may understand My statutes and learn to love My instructions more than gold.

You will also learn to consider all of My precepts because they are right, and as a result you will hate every wrong way, therefore, the enemy would not be able to outwit you, the enemy will have no dominion over you because you will be able to recognize all of his devices and use the wisdom I will give you as you study My word, and begin to put it into practice for your life (Psalm 119:121-128)!!

Love,

I Am your Discernment and Understanding

POINTS TO CONSIDER

1. When you do what is right Father will not allow anyone to oppress you.

2. He will be your vindicator and He will vindicate you from your enemies who rise up against you.

3. Know that His love for you is great.

4. Father wants to teach you His ways because He wants you to know who He really is.

5. He will give you discernment so you will not be ignorant of the devil's devices.

6. Purpose in your heart to practice His presence on a daily basis.

7. Know that discernment and understanding comes only form Him.

♥ *BE ENCOURAGED TODAY MY LOVE* ♥

♥♣♥

My love,

I want you to be quick to listen, slow to speak and slow to get angry, for human anger does not bring about the righteous life that I desire. Therefore, get rid of all moral filth and the evil that is so prevalent, and humbly accept the word planted in your heart, which can save your soul.

My love; do not merely listen to My word, and so deceive yourself. Do what it says. Anyone who listens to My word but does not do what it says; is like a person who looks at their face in a mirror and after looking at themselves, goes away and immediately forgets what they looked like. But the person who looks intently into the perfect law that gives freedom, and continues to do this, not forgetting what they have heard, but doing it—they will be blessed in what they do.

My love, anyone who considers themselves religious, yet does not keep a tight rein on their tongue deceives themselves and their religion is worthless.

Religion that I accept is pure and faultless; it is to look after orphans and widows in their distress, and to keep oneself from being polluted by the world (James 1:19-27)

Love,

I Am the One who teaches you to be pure and faultless

POINTS TO CONSIDER

1. Don't merely listen to the word, and so deceive yourself. Do what it says.

2. Remember faith without works is dead, so learn to walk it out.

3. If you listen to the word and don't do what it says you are only fooling yourself.

4. Look intently into the perfect law that gives freedom, and do not forget what you have heard and you will be blessed in what you do.

5. Watch your words; anyone who considers themselves Christ like and yet does not keep a tight rein on their tongue deceives themselves and their religion is worthless.

6. True Christianity God accepts; is pure and faultless, it keeps oneself from being polluted by the world, and takes care of those in need.

7. Father will teach you to become pure and faultless as you continue to draw closer to Him.

BE ENCOURAGED TODAY MY LOVE

My Love,

I want you to follow My example in everything you do and live a life filled with love for others.

Be reminded that I have loved you with an everlasting love.

My love, when you obey My instructions you will remain in My love, just as I obeyed My Father's and remained in His love. My love, "If you want a life of love, joy, peace, prosperity and success" you must love others. Remember I have command you to love others as I have loved you.

My love, those who obey Me will become My friends.

Do you want to be a friend of mine? You will become My friend when you begin to read, believe, meditate, and practice My written word (Ephesians 5:1&2; John 15:9-13&14)!

Love,

I Am your Friend

POINTS TO CONSIDER

1. Imitate God in everything you do.

2. Love others as Jesus loves you.

3. When you practice His presence you will remain in His love, and He will call you friend.

4. If you want things to go well for you, you must practice the love of Jesus.

5. Be reminded that those who are willing and obedient will enjoy many benefits.

6. Remember, love is not a suggestion, it's a commandment.

7. Father's greatest desire is to be able to call you friend.

BE ENCOURAGED TODAY MY LOVE

My love,

Be reminded My love, My word is full of living power, it is sharper than the sharpest knife and it cuts deep into the innermost thoughts and desires.

My love when you fast don't make it obvious like the hypocrites do, they try to look pale and disheveled so people will admire them for their fasting!

I, My love, will anoint you with fresh oil more than those you associate with as you continue to keep My ways. You also need to know My love, that praying My written word will give you instructions in doing what is right, Just and fair, and as you continue to worship, adore, admire and appreciate Me with all your heart, soul, mind and strength, I will give you strength to war in the spirit.

I will make you like a tree planted by the rivers of water which brings forth fruit in season. Your leaves will not wither and whatever you do will prosper, because you do not compromise your godly standards.

Be encouraged today My love, knowing that I Am with you always.

(Matt 6:16; Psalm 1:3; 45:7; 144:1; Proverbs 1:3; Hebrews 4:12)

Love,

I Am your Adviser

POINTS TO CONSIDER

1. Father wants you to know that He will cause you to bear much fruit because of your obedience to Him.

2. Everything you set forth your hands to do will prosper because you stay in covenant relationship with Him.

3. When you set aside time to pray, fast and seek His face it should be kept private between you and Him.

4. He will give you a fresh new anointing to carry His glory.

5. Pray the scriptures, they are powerful, alive, sharp and active, and they accomplish His purposes.

6. Purpose in your heart to become more of a worshiper.

7. Know that the Lord is your adviser and best friend, the One who sticks closer than a brother.

BE ENCOURAGED TODAY MY LOVE

My love,

Don't be double-minded but learn to trust Me without wavering, remember I Am your Refuge and Strength, so put your hope in Me by reading, believing, meditating in, and practicing My written word.

My love, I also want you to stay away from evildoers, those who practice a lifestyle of sin, so that you may learn to keep all of My commandments and follow My instructions. I, My love will sustain you according to My promises, and your hopes will be satisfied.

I will uphold you so you will always have regard for My instructions.

My love, as you do what is right, I will not allow your enemies to triumph over you, and I will continuously look over your well being, so the arrogant will not oppress you, and when you allow My gentle spirit to lead you My love, you will have My guaranteed benefits.

(Psalm119: 113-122)

Love,

I Am your Guaranteed Benefits

POINTS TO CONSIDER

1. Don't be double minded, Father wants you to be single minded about spiritual things.

2. Put your hope and trust in Him.

3. He wants you to stay away from those who practice a lifestyle of sin, because bad company corrupts good habit.

4. He will keep His promises made to you; know that He is completing the good work He had begun in you.

5. Remember that He is with you always, and the enemy will not have dominion over your life.

6. Allow His gentle spirit to lead you, and you will receive His guaranteed benefits.

7. Be reminded that the Lord is your benefit package.

BE ENCOURAGED TODAY MY LOVE

My love,

My precious one, I want you to know that My words are more precious than gold, than much pure gold. They are sweeter than honey, than honey from the comb and as you learn to read, believe, meditate and practice My holy word, you, My love would be fed with the finest wheat; with honey from the rock I will satisfy you, and as you continue to meditate in My word and practice what you have learned daily they will become sweeter than honey to your taste!

My love, My words will also equip you to speak pleasant words which will bring joy, comfort, hope and peace to those who are downtrodden, because pleasant words are like a honeycomb, sweet to the soul, and healing to the bones. My love, My darling, My desire is that your lips will drip with sweetness as the honeycomb.

My bride; you also need to know that I have equipped you with milk and honey that are under your tongue, because I chose you in Christ Jesus even before I made the world, to live holy, and when you make the wise choice to follow My instructions and live holy by drawing closer to Me, and staying connected to the vine "Jesus," the fragrance of your garments will be like that of Lebanon.

Be reminded My love, My word is a lamp to your feet that lights your path!!

Psalm 19:10; Psalm 81:16; Psalm 119:103; Proverbs 16:24; Song of Solomon 4:11!

Love,

I Am your Honey in the Rock

POINTS TO CONSIDER

1. Father wants you to know Him through His word so that honey, His sweetness can be activated in your life.

2. Know that Jesus is your honey in the rock, so listen to His teachings and build your life on the solid foundation of His word.

3. As a result you will speak pure words, sweet words. Your words will bring forth life, healing and health.

4. You need to remember that you are the Bride of Christ, since you are a part of the body of Christ, so learn to behave like a happy bride.

5. If you have ever been married you remember how special your wedding day was just being the bride, well, it's the same concept, that's the way your bridegroom sees you every day as special.

6. You have already been equipped with milk and honey under your tongue, so speak pure words.

7. Follow the Lord's instructions and live holy.

BE ENCOURAGED TODAY MY LOVE

My Love,

I want you to be humble and gentle, and make allowance for the faults of others because of your love for Me. Live a life filled with love for others following the example of Christ who loved you and gave Himself as a sacrifice to take away your sins.

My love, I also want you to know that My grace and peace is always with you, so don't live the way you used to before you accepted Christ Jesus as Lord and Savior of your life.

My love, allow My Gentle Spirit to lead you, live in the light and follow My instructions; practice obedience to My word and it will make you wise.

My love, you need to know that I have set you apart as a vessel of honor to be used to carry My glory throughout the earth.

(Ephesians1:2; 2:2; 4:2&5:2)!

Love,

I Am your Humility

POINTS TO CONSIDER

1. The Lord wants you to know that His Gentle Spirit is always with you.

2. Remember to live the new life, live in the light, practice holiness, and purpose in your heart to become a person of integrity.

3. Be humble and gentle; make allowance for the faults of others. Practice the "Golden Rule," and treat others the way you would like to be treated.

4. Follow the example of Jesus who loved you and gave His life as a sacrifice to take away your sins.

5. Father honors you, He has set you apart to carry His glory, so set aside time so you can hear His voice clearly to move on and do what He has called you to do.

6. Humble yourself in the sight of the Lord, and He will exalt you in due season.

7. Remember the meek will inherit the earth and receive God's abundance.

♥♥ *BE ENCOURAGED TODAY MY LOVE* ♥♥
♥‡♥

My love

You need to know that I extend My perfect peace and mercy towards you everyday!

My precious daughter, you need to know that I have given you freedom through the death and resurrection of My Son Jesus Christ who is your restoration.

You also need to know that He is the One who teaches you compassion and gives you the glorious privilege of coming to know Me as Lord.

My love, I want you to learn to trust Me, and rest in My love for you, being reminded that I Am your Eternal Life Giver, Life in the Spirit, Covenant Keeper, Cry for Help, your Rescue, and your Radiance and Joy.

Be encouraged today My love, be brave and courageous, knowing that I Am your trusted friend. So continue to trust Me with all of your heart and not lean on your own understanding, but acknowledge Me in all your ways, and I will direct your path. (Proverbs 3:5&6; Psalm 121).

Love,

I Am Your Trusted Friend

POINTS TO CONSIDER

1. Father wants you to know that He extends peace and mercy towards you every day, He does things for you that you sometimes are not even aware of.

2. He also wants you to know that He had set you free from the yoke of bondage to sin when you accepted Jesus Christ as Lord and savior of your life.

3. You also need to know He is the One who teaches you compassion and gives you the glorious privilege of coming to know Jesus as Lord.

4. Learn to trust Him completely.

5. Learn to rest in His great love for you.

6. Be brave and courageous; remember He is a friend who sticks closer than a brother.

7. Trust Him with all your heart, and allow Him to lead you along the right paths for your life.

BE ENCOURAGED TODAY MY LOVE

My love,

I will give you the strength as a wild ox, and anoint you with the finest oil so you can become as surefooted as a deer which stands upon mountain heights without any fear of evil. You My love will become secure and confident in My great love and protection for you.

You need to know My love that My words are pure, My promises are truth and they serve as a shield to you and all those who put their trust in Me, so continue to rest in Me My love, as you learn to trust Me with all of your heart, soul, mind and strength.

You My love are like a lily among thorns.

My love, I have anointed you more than those you associate with because you love what is good and hate what is evil, so arise and shine for all to see, and though the people walk around in darkness, My glory has arisen over you, because I have anointed you to preach the Good News, to set at liberty those who are bound up, so you can bring freedom and liberty to the captives.

I also want you to know My love, that I Am always with you. I will never leave nor forsake you because I Am your God; and your times are in My hands.

My love, I will comfort you, I will help you, and I will uphold you with My right hand.

You My love are next in line for a miracle.
(Psalm 18:33; 45:7; 92:10& 18:33)!

Love,

I Am your Only True Love.

POINTS TO CONSIDER

1. Father wants you to know that He will equip you with the strength you need to fulfill purpose, and He will anoint you with an anointing that no one else can copy or emulate because you are very precious to Him.

2. He has set you apart to carry His glory.

3. He wants you to arise and shine for all to see.

4. Believe in Him, believe His word; believe in His promises because they are truth, pure, and they are perfect.

5. He also wants you to preach the good news of the gospel of Jesus Christ to set at liberty those who are bound up, so the captives can be set free.

6. Be reminded that He is always with you.

7. Know that your times are in His hands, and every day of your life is recorded in His book.

BE ENCOURAGED TODAY MY LOVE

My love,

My love I will bless you when you persevere under trials, because when you have stood the test, you will receive the crown of life that I have promised to those who love Me.

So consider it pure joy, whenever you face trials of many kinds, because you know that the testing of your faith develops perseverance. Perseverance must finish its work so that you may be mature and complete, not lacking anything.

My love, if you lack wisdom, ask Me, and I will give you generously without finding fault, but when you ask, you must believe and not doubt, because those who doubt is like a wave of the sea, blown and tossed by the wind. Don't think you will receive anything from Me because a double minded person is unstable in all of their ways.

My love, when you are tempted to do wrong never say that I Am tempting you, for I cannot temp you with evil, when you are tempted to do evil it is because you are drawn away by your own evil desires and evil desires gives birth to sin, so never say I Am tempting you when you do wrong, because "I AM Holy" and there is no unrighteousness in Me!!

(James 1:1-8 &12-15)

Love,

I Am the One Who delivers you from temptation

POINTS TO CONSIDER

1. Consider it pure joy, whenever you face trials of many kinds, because you know that the testing of your faith develops perseverance, and perseverance must finish its work so that you may be mature and complete, not lacking anything.

2. Know that your trials comes to make you strong so you can move on to the next level in God, they will equip you with the strength and wisdom you will need for the next step in destiny.

3. Father will bless you when you persevere under trials, because when you have stood the test, you will receive the crown of life.

4. Remember when you are tempted to do wrong never say that God is tempting you, for He is holy, and He cannot and will not temp you with evil.

5. Know that Papa is holy and there is no unrighteousness in Him.

6. Remember He is the one who delivers you from all temptations.

7. So continue to seek first His kingdom and righteousness, and grow in wisdom, knowledge and understanding of who He really is!!

BE ENCOURAGED TODAY MY LOVE

My love,

I want you to know that it is My peace which gives you hope, it's the kind of peace that surpasses all human understanding, it cannot be obtained from anyone, or anywhere else, and as you continue to allow My gentle spirit to lead you, you will continue to experience My perfect peace, so I urge you to seek peace and pursue it, as it will guard your heart and mind.

My love, when you begin to trust Me with all your heart and stop leaning on your own understanding, you will have peace like a river which will flood your soul, and as you build your life on the solid foundation of My word, you will continue to experience great peace even when everyone or everything else is falling apart around you, peace like a river will flood your soul, because you have learned to trust Me in every area of your life.

My love, I will give you roots that grows deep down into the water, like the tree planted by the riverbank which long months of drought cannot disturb.

My precious daughter, know that I Am always with you, and I Am your Prince of Peace (Psalm 29:11; 34:14; Matthew 7:23&24; Jeremiah 17:7&8)!

Love,

I Am your Prince of Peace

POINTS TO CONSIDER

1. Father wants you to know that His peace will give you hope.

2. His peace surpasses all human understanding.

3. Allow His gentle Spirit to lead you, and you will experience perfect peace.

4. Learn to trust Him with all your heart and stop leaning on your own understanding.

5. Build your life on the solid foundation of His word so you can stand strong.

6. You will become like the tree on the riverbank which long months of drought will not disturb.

7. Remember the Lord is your Prince of Peace.

♥*BE ENCOURAGED TODAY MY LOVE*♥

My Love,

I have created My House to be a house of prayer for all nations; however, the wicked have made it into a den of thieves! The sins of My people are so gross that they have been separated from Me.

I will not listen to their prayers anymore, there hands are hands of murderers, they continue to kill the innocent every day by the billions throughout the nations, their fingers are filthy with sin, their mouths are filled with lies and tainted with corruption, and sexual immorality are running rampant in the lands!

All this I have seen and I cannot keep silent much longer, I continue to wait for people to come to Me in repentance, however, they refuse, and they continue on in their sinful, rebellious ways, while they think I don't see what they are doing; however, I will rebuke the nations for their iniquity and set things in order.

My love, people seem to forget that I Am the one who made the eyes; and I see everything, I Am the one who made the ears and I hear everything! I Am the one who made them even before I placed them in the womb; however they think I am not aware of their behavior.

Be reminded My love, that I know and see all things and I patiently wait for people to turn from their sins!!

(Isaiah 1: 1-9; 56:7; 57:2; Matt 31:13; Mark11:17; Luke19:46; Psalm 51:20)!

Love,

I Know and See All Things

POINTS TO CONSIDER

1. Father wants you to know that there are a lot of wolves in sheep's clothing in His house; so watch and pray.

2. His people have turned His house into a den of thieves and robbers.

3. The sins of the people have separated them from the Lord.

4. He continues to wait with His arms wide open for people to come to Him in repentance (Isaiah 1:18).

5. Be reminded; He sits on the circles of the earth, and He know and sees all things. Everything that goes on in the earth.

6. People need to repent and turn from their wicked ways.

7. Judgment will be executed if people don't wake up from their slumber and know who God really is, and begin to cry out in repentance so He can heal the Land!!

BE ENCOURAGED TODAY MY LOVE

My Love,

My precious daughter, I want you to remember that Jesus is the Vine; and I Am the vinedresser, and when you stay connected to the Vine you would be richly blessed.

You will become like a tree planted along the river bank, with roots that reaches deep into the water, such trees are not bothered by the heat, nor worried by long months of drought, their leaves stay green and they go right on producing delicious fruits.

My love, I want you to stay connected to the vine by cultivating your relationship with Jesus.

You cultivate your relationship with Him by following His teachings, so you must read and meditate in the holy bible day and night; allow the word to dwell in you richly so you can become wise, and as a result you will edify, build up and encourage others, and self. So learn to represent Him well.

Practice the Love of Jesus; do not take ungodly counsel, live in the light, and stay alive in Him. Have an overwhelming desire to live holy at all times, and allow the fruit of the spirit to be evident in your life.

My love, stay planted in the good soil where there will be plenty of water, so you can grow into a splendid tree, which will produce rich leaves and luscious fruits, and as you stay in My love, you will become a fruitful olive tree where the birds of the air will come and nest in your branches! That means the people of the world will come to you for advice and instructions for their lives, because they will know that My life's blood flows through you.

(Jeremiah 17:7&8; Ezekiel 17:8); Mark13:32)!

Love,

I Am your Vinedresser

POINTS TO CONSIDER

1. Build your life on the solid foundation of God's word.

2. Listen to the teachings of Jesus and stay connected Him.

3. Purpose in your heart to become like the fruitful tree planted by the river bank.

4. Practice the love of Jesus; learn to imitate Him in everything you do.

5. Do not take ungodly counsel.

6. Stay planted in the good soil where there will be plenty of water, so you can grow into a splendid tree, which will produce rich leaves and luscious fruits.

7. You will become a fruitful olive tree, and the birds of the air will come and nest in your branches. That means; the people of the world will come to you for advice and instruction for their lives, because they will know that God's Holy Spirit, the spirit of wisdom lives inside of you!

BE ENCOURAGED TODAY MY LOVE

My love,

I want you to make Me your priority number One, because I Am your Creator and Eternal Guide, remember I have crated you in My image, after My likeness and called you My masterpiece.

I also want you know My love; that I will guide to into all truth, so learn to listen for My instructions while being reminded that I Am your Commander and Chief in battle.

My love, you will experience great joy as you learn to walk in integrity and exercise your faith in Me. Remember that My way is perfect. I also want you to know that My protective shield is round about you, so continue to listen for My all powerful voice, knowing that I will always be your help in times of trouble.

I, My love, will provide for you because I Am your Creator who cares deeply for you. So remember that I Am your Teacher, Intercessor, Everlasting Kindness, Discernment and Trusted Friend.

My love, I Am your Divine Instructor, Cry for help, Devine Provider, and your Creator who cares deeply for you. I Am your Teacher and Intercessor, Everlasting Kindness, Romance and Eternity!!

Love,

I will provide for you

POINTS TO CONSIDER

1. Father wants you to make Him priority number One in your life.

2. Remember He created you in His image and called you His masterpiece.

3. Learn to listen to His instructions and He will lead and guide you into all truths.

4. Remember His ways are perfect.

5. He will provide for you because He cares deeply for you.

6. He is your Divine Instructor, Cry for help, Devine Provider, and your Creator who cares deeply for you. He's your Teacher and Intercessor, Everlasting Kindness, Romance and Eternity.

7. Remember He is your Everything!!

BE ENCOURAGED TODAY MY LOVE

My love,

When you pray, I want you to pray My will to be done in every situation, and in every area of your life, and when you cry out to Me I will hear and answer you, and deliver you from all of your troubles.

My love, you need to know that I Am a Shield for you, the Glory and the lifter of your head. You also need to know and be assured that when you cry out to Me, I will listen and answer you, because I hear you when you pray, and I pay attention to your groaning and listen to your cry for help.

My love, please know that because of My unfailing love for you, you can enter My house with deepest awe and worship Me in sprit and truth. I will listen to your voice in the morning, each morning as you bring your request to Me and wait expectantly.

My love, I also want you to know that I bless those who live holy, I surround them with My shield of love, and the fruit of My spirit is evident in their lives, so take refuge in Me My love and learn to rejoice singing joyful praises forever and ever!

(Matt 6:10; Psalm 3:3,4;5:1,2 & 3,7,11& 22 &34:6)!

Love,

I Am your Refuge

POINTS TO CONSIDER

1. Father wants you to pray His will be done in your situations.

2. Know that He is a shield for you, and He will protect you from the wicked.

3. When you pray He will listen and answer your prayers.

4. Remember to come boldly before the throne of grace to find help in your time of need.

5. Learn to trust in the Lord with all your heart, exercise your faith and trust Him completely.

6. When you live according the God's ways you will enjoy many, many benefits.

7. Learn to cast all of your cares upon Him, remember He cares deeply for you.

BE ENCOURAGED TODAY MY LOVE

My love,

I want you to be joyful always—rejoice! Let everyone see that you are considerate in all you do, and remember that I Am coming soon.

My love, don't worry about anything; instead, pray about everything. Tell Me what you need, and thank Me for all I have done, then you will experience My perfect peace, which exceeds anything you can understand. My love, My peace will guard your heart and mind as you live in Christ Jesus, practicing His presence.

I also want you to know, My dear, darling daughter, one final thing. Fix your thoughts on what is true, and honorable, and right, and pure, and lovely, and admirable.

Think about things that are excellent and worthy of praise. Keep putting into practice all you have learned and received from Me . . . everything you heard from Me and saw Me doing through My son Jesus . . . . Then My peace will be with you always. (Philippians 4:4-9)

Love,

I Am your Peace forever

POINTS TO CONSIDER

1. Be joyful always; learn to rejoice in God's goodness.

2. Let everyone see that you are considerate in all you do.

3. Remember, Jesus is coming soon.

4. Don't worry about anything.

5. Pray about everything.

6. Tell Father what you want.

7. Thank Him for all He has done so you can experience His perfect peace, which exceeds anything you can understand, and be reminded that thankfulness is a sacrifice that truly pleases Him.

BE ENCOURAGED TODAY MY LOVE

My love,

I want you to become the wise woman I have called you to be, one who would build her house, and not tear it down with her hands like the foolish woman does.

Please know My love, that I have already equipped you with everything you will ever need to walk in wisdom, and when you feel like you lack wisdom you need to ask Me because I give liberally to all those who ask of Me; so I encourage you My love, to meditate in My written word day and night for a life of prosperity and success, so that My word will dwell richly in you, and as a result you will be able to encourage, edify, and builds up others and yourself!

My desire is that you will become like a tree planted by the rivers of water, which brings forth fruit in season, where your leaves will not wither so whatever you do will prosper.

My love, I want you to purpose in your heart to leave your sinful ways behind and stop looking at worthless things, stop wasting time on meaningless things and remind yourself that you are a representative of Jesus Christ, and you need to represent Him well in all you say or do.

So I encourage you My love, to build your life with the wisdom that comes only from Me, not human wisdom (Proverbs9:6;14:1;Col3:16&17;Ps1:3&Joshua1:8)!

Love,

I Am your Life Planner & Counselor

POINTS TO CONSIDER

1. Be the wise woman Father has called you to be, one who would build and not tear down.

2. Know that Father has already equipped you with everything you will ever need to walk in wisdom.

3. When you feel like you lack wisdom you need to ask Him.

4. True wisdom comes only from Him.

5. Let the Word of Christ dwell richly in you, it will make you wise.

6. Wisdom will cause you to make wise choices for your life.

7. You will also be equipped to encourage, edify, and build up others and yourself!

BE ENCOURAGED TODAY MY LOVE

My love,

You need to know that prayer is your key to victory. You also need to know My love that My word opens gates where only the righteous can enter with thanksgiving; it opens gates that leads into My presence and only the godly can enter there.

My love, My precious daughter, I want you to put on salvation as a helmet, and use the sword of the spirit which is My written word, and be reminded My love, that your fight is not against flesh and blood enemies but against evil rulers and authorities in the unseen world, against those mighty powers of darkness who rule this world, and against wicked spirits in the heavenly realm.

My love, you must use every piece of My armor to resist the enemy, you must wear the sturdy belt of truth as the body's armor of righteousness; that means you must know My word and live a life of holiness, as you cannot win any battles if you continue to live in carnality. So I encourage you My love, to pray at all times, use the mighty powerful gift I have given you, and pray My word is every situation.

(Psalm 118:19; Ephesians 6:12, 13, 17&18)

Love,

I Am the One who prepares you for battle

POINTS TO CONSIDER

1. Know that prayer is your key to all victory.

2. Father also wants you to know that His word opens gates where only the righteous can enter with thanksgiving; it opens gates that lead to His presence.

3. He wants you to live holy and learn to use His word in your situations because His word is alive, powerful, sharp and active. It destroys principalities, powers, and evil and wicked spirits that are on assignment to destroy your life.

4. Learn to use every piece of the armor to resist the enemy.

5. Know the truth; it will make you strong in your faith.

6. Live a life of holiness as you cannot win any battles if you continue to live in sin.

7. Pray at all times, use the mighty powerful gift God has given you so you can fight every battle and win.

BE ENCOURAGED TODAY MY LOVE

My love,

Your life would be joyful and happy when you begin to practice My presence by following My instructions because of your love and reverence for Me.

You My love; will enjoy the fruit of your labor, how joyful and prosperous you will be!

You will be like a fruitful grapevine flourishing within your home. Your children will be like vigorous young olive trees as they sit around your table.

My love; these are My blessing for all those who fear Me, those who love, adore, worship, reverence and appreciate Me. My love, I will continue to bless you from Zion.

I will bless you with long and satisfying life, and you will live to enjoy your grandchildren and experience great peace (Psalm 128)!

Love,

I Am your Fruitful Grapevine

POINTS TO CONSIDER

1. Father wants you to know that your life will be joyful and happy when you begin to practice His presence.

2. Learn to follow His instructions because you love Him.

3. You will enjoy the fruit of your labor.

4. The Lord will give you prosperity.

5. You will become a fruitful grapevine flourishing within your home.

6. Your children will be successful.

7. You will live to enjoy your grand-children.

BE ENCOURAGED TODAY MY LOVE

My love,

It is very important to work hard to show the results of your salvation by obeying My instructions with deep reverence and fear, know that I Am working in you, and giving you the desires and the power to do what pleases Me the most!

My love, I want you to do everything without complaining and murmuring, so that no one can criticize you. Live a clean and innocent life as My holy, beloved daughter, shining like a bright light in a world full of crooked and perverse people. Hold firmly to the word of life; then on the day of Christ's return you will be proud that you did not run the race in vain, and that your work was not useless.

My love, watch out for the dogs, those people who do evil, those mutilators who say you must be circumcised to be saved; for those who worship by My Spirit are the ones who are truly circumcised. They rely on what Christ Jesus has done for them. My love put no confidence in human effort (Philippians 2:12-18&3:2-4)

Love,

I Am your Confidence

POINTS TO CONSIDER

1. Work hard to show the results of your salvation by obeying God's instructions.

2. Have a strong desire to do what pleases Him.

3. Do everything without complaining and murmuring, so that no one can criticize you.

4. Live a clean and innocent life, shining like a bright light in a world full of crooked and perverse people.

5. Hold firmly to the word of life; then, on the day of Christ's return you will be proud that you did not run the race in vain, and that your work was not useless.

6. Watch out for the dogs, those people who do evil.

7. Rely on what Christ Jesus has done for you, and do not put confidence in human beings, trust in the Lord always!

♥ BE ENCOURAGED TODAY MY LOVE ♥

My love,

When you offer up your praises with a sacrifice of thanksgiving to Me; I will rescue you. I will not allow your enemies to triumph over you. And when you cry out to Me for help, I will restore your health. I, My love will keep you from falling into the pit of death.

Continue to sing praises to Me My love, offer up praises and praise My holy name!

Remember My anger lasts only a moment, but My favor lasts a lifetime. Weeping may last through the night, but joy comes with the morning.

My love, My favor will make you as secure as a mountain. If I turn away from you, you will be shattered. Remember I Am where all of your help comes from. I Am the One who helps you in all of your troubles. I Am the one who turns your mourning into joyful dancing and take away your clothes of mourning, and I clothed you with joy, that you might sing praises to Me and not be silent so you may continue to thank Me forever (Psalm 30:1-2&11-12)!

Love,

My favor lasts a lifetime

POINTS TO CONSIDER

1. Purpose in your heart to offer up praises with thanksgiving to the King of Kings, and Lord of Lords.

2. Father will not allow your enemies to triumph over you.

3. Know that praise is your weapon of warfare.

4. He will restore your health when sickness comes upon you.

5. His favor will make you secure as a mountain.

6. He will turn your morning into joyful dancing and clothe you with joy.

7. Purpose in your heart to become more of a worshiper.

♥BE ENCOURAGED TODAY MY LOVE♥

♥☦♥

My love,

You need to know that I Am your Trust and Protection, your Papa who knows and sees all things. I Am your Help and Rescue, so continue to look to Me, for I Am where all of your help comes from. My love, I Am your Shield, Glory and the Lifter of your head, and I keep a protective shield round about you, so be reminded that I Am your Vindicator, Peace and Safety.

My love, I Am the one who hears and answers all of your prayers, so live by My power, knowing that I Am your Living Light, the one who teaches you how to love and wants to spend precious time with you.

My love, I want you to watch and pray, and I will give you everlasting peace, so learn to trust Me and I will anoint your head with fresh oil. Be reminded that I Am your Shepherd, so allow Me to lead you into green pastures as you seek My wisdom and direction, and learn to rest in My love for you.

Love,

I Am your Rest

POINTS TO CONSIDER

1. Father wants you to learn to rest in His love for you.

2. Know that He is your Trust and Protection.

3. He wants you to live by His power.

4. He hears your cry for help and will answer, just be patient as you continue to seek first His kingdom, and live holy.

5. Ask Him for wisdom, understanding and direction in all your situations.

6. Allow Him to lead you like the shepherd leads the sheep.

7. Know that He always wants to spend precious time with you.

BE ENCOURAGED TODAY MY LOVE

My love,

I want you to rejoice in My strength for you, and you will have great joy in the victories I give! I will grant you the desires of your heart and not withhold the request of your lips.

My love, I will welcome you with rich blessings, and place a crown of pure gold upon your head, you asked for life and I gave it to you with length of days forever and ever when you accepted Jesus as Lord and Savior of your life!!

My love, I will give you victory and make your glory great; I will bestowed on you My splendor and majesty, for surely I will grant you eternal blessings and make you glad with the joy of My presence; and when you trust in Me, My unfailing love for you will never be shaken.

My love, My hand will lay hold on all your enemies; My right hand will seize your foes, and at the time of My appearing I will make them like a fiery furnace in My wrath. I the LORD will swallow them up and My fire will consume them.

My love, though they plot evil against you and devise wicked schemes, they cannot succeed; for I will make them turn their backs when I aim at them with drawn bow.

My love, learn to sing praises to Me with all of your heart (Psalm 21)!!

Love,

I Am the Exalted One

POINTS TO CONSIDER

1. Rejoice in the Lord and you will have great joy in the victories He gives.

2. He will grant you the desires of your heart and not withhold the request of your lips.

3. The Lord will welcome you with rich blessings, and place a crown of pure gold on your head.

4. He will give you victory always and make your glory great.

5. He will bestow on you His splendor and majesty.

6. When you trust in the Lord, His unfailing love for you will never be shaken.

7. His hand will lay hold on all your enemies; His right hand will seize your foes.

BE ENCOURAGED TODAY MY LOVE

My Love,

I want you to learn to rejoice in confident hope, be patient in trouble and keep on praying. I will come with great power and rescue you, and I will defend you with My mighty arm!

Be reminded My love, that I Am your Wisdom and Deliverer, your Light and Salvation; and your Fortress who protects you from all danger, so remain in My love being reminded that I Am your Lover and True Friend.

My love, don't worry about the wicked, or envy those who do wrong, for like the grass they will soon fade away, like spring flowers they will wither away.

You also need to know My love, that fools says in their heart's there is no God, I don't exist, they are corrupt and their actions are evil, so as a result they don't know Me, they don't know Who I really Am, so they don't know how to do anything right.

My love, My precious one; don't worry about the wicked, and remember, I Am with you always (Romans 12:12; Psalm 14:1; 27:1; 37:1&2; 54:1; 121:3; John15:9)!

Love,

I Am with you always

POINTS TO CONSIDER

1. Learn to rejoice in confident hope.

2. Be patient in trouble and keep on praying.

3. Know that the Lord will come with great power and rescue you. He will make your enemies powerless against you.

4. Don't worry about the wicked, or envy those who do wrong, for like the grass they will soon fade away, like spring flowers they will wither away.

5. Only the fool says God don't exist because their hearts are hardened.

6. Remember God is with you always.

7. Know that the Lord is your Wisdom and Deliverer.

BE ENCOURAGED TODAY MY LOVE

My love,

Be reminded that the earth is Mine, and everything in it, the world, and all who lives in it; for I founded it upon the seas and established it upon the waters, and only those who love Me and follow My instructions may live in My holy place.

Those who have clean hands; and a pure heart. Those who do not lift up their souls to idols or swear by what is false, they will receive My blessings and vindication because they seek first My kingdom and righteousness.

My love, continue to lift up your head, and I, the King of glory will come in.

Remember, I Am the King of glory, your Lord strong and mighty, the One mighty in battle (Psalm 24)!

Love,

I Am your King of Glory

POINTS TO CONSIDER

1. Be reminded that the earth is the Lord's and everything in it, the world, and all who lives in it.

2. Only those who love Him and follow His instructions will stand in His holy place.

3. Only those with clean hands; and a pure heart will see God's face.

4. Continue to draw close to the Lord and He will draw closer to you.

5. Remember the Lord is the King of glory.

6. He alone is strong and mighty.

7. He alone is mighty in battle.

BE ENCOURAGED TODAY MY LOVE

My love,

I want you to know that I bless those who live holy, and I surround them with My shield of love, so as a result; the fruit of My spirit is evident in their lives. My love, learn to take refuge in Me, and you will learn to rejoice and sing joyful praises, and when you pray I will bend down and listen!

My love, when My people who are called by My name, begins to humble themselves and pray, seek My face and turn from their wicked ways, I will hear from heaven, forgive their sins and heal the land. Then My ears and My eyes will be opened, and I will be attentive to every prayer they pray, and though their sins are like crimson I shall make them as white as snow.

My love, when you begin to pray My word, you will learn that I Am righteous and My decisions are fair, My instructions are perfect and entirely trustworthy.

(Psalm 5:11, 12; 17:6; 119:137&138; Galatians 5:22; 2 Chronicles 7:14&15 & Isaiah 1:18)!

Love,

I will surround you with My shield of love

POINTS TO CONSIDER

1. Father will bless you when you live holy.

2. He will surround you with His shield of love.

3. The fruit of the spirit would be evident in your life.

4. Learn to take refuge in Him.

5. Learn to rejoice and sing Him joyful praises.

6. Know that when you pray He will bend down and listen.

7. He will surround you with His shield of love.

BE ENCOURAGED TODAY MY LOVE

My love,

You have heard that it was said, 'love your neighbor and hate your enemy." But I tell you: Love your enemies and pray for those who persecute you, that by your love the world will know that you are My disciple.

My love, My desire is that My people everywhere would lift up holy hands in prayer, without anger or disputing, and pray for all people everywhere.

I urge, then first of all, that requests, prayers, intercession and thanksgiving be made for everyone—for kings and all those in authority. Pray that they would be worthy of the calling I have placed upon them, and that they will have a heart I can use, so that My people may live peaceful and quiet lives in all godliness and holiness, for this is good and it pleases Me your Savior, who wants all people to be saved and come to the knowledge of the truth.

My love, pray for those who are lost. Intercede for everyone.

(Matt 5:43-44; 1Timothy2:1-4&8; Ephesians 6:18)!

Love,

I want all people to be saved

POINTS TO CONSIDER

1. The Lord wants you to love your enemies.

2. Become a true disciple by praying for your enemies.

3. He desires that people everywhere would lift up holy hands in prayer everywhere without doubting or disputing.

4. Pray for kings and all those in authority.

5. Pray that they would be worthy of the calling of the Lord, and they will take their responsibilities seriously.

6. He wants all people to be saved.

7. Intercede for everyone.

BE ENCOURAGED TODAY MY LOVE

My Love,

I want you to know that those who love Me are guided by their honesty; however, the treacherous are destroyed by their dishonesty!

My love, you need to learn to commit your ways to Me, for only then your plans will succeed.

Don't be like the teachers of religious laws, the Pharisees and hypocrites, they are like white washed tombs, beautiful on the outside but are filled on the inside with dead men bones and all sorts of impurity, they try to look upright to people on the outside but inside their hearts are filled with hypocrisy and lawlessness.

Learn to love others as I have loved you through My son Jesus. Don't be judgmental, remember, you look at the outward appearance but I look at the heart, I weight the thoughts and intentions of everyone.

My precious daughter, I want you to draw close to Me and I will draw closer to you, have a desire to know Me more intimately, worship and serve Me with your whole heart and a willing mind, for I see every heart and know and understand every plan and thought. My love, if you seek for Me you will find Me, however if you forsake Me, I will reject you forever so take My word seriously!

My love, do not be like the people of the nations, the un-regenerated, those who do not walk in a love relationship with Me, and everything they offer is defiled.

My love, let love be your highest goal, desire to become a woman of integrity, purpose to become like a tree planted by the rivers of water which brings forth fruit in season; where your leaves will not wither and whatever you do will prosper.

(Psalm 1; Proverbs 11:3; Proverbs 16:2; Matthew 23:27-28; 1Samuel 16:7);
(John 13; 34;1Chronicles 28:9;Haggai 2:15)!

Love,

I Am your Uprightness and Integrity

POINTS TO CONSIDER

1. When you stay in covenant relationship with the Lord He will lead you in the way you should go and guide you with His eyes.

2. Commit your ways to Him and all of your plans will succeed.

3. The Lord wants you to be beautiful from the inside out, not just on the outside.

4. Let love be your highest goal.

5. Father desires true worship from you.

6. Purpose in your heart to live a life of holiness, a life that pleases Him.

7. Desire to become a fruit bearing tree, and practice integrity.

BE ENCOURAGED TODAY MY LOVE

My love,

You need to begin your day with praise, worship, adoration and thanksgiving.

Learn to glorify My Holy name as you begin your day My love. This should be followed by praying the scriptures as they will give you hope and comfort for each day. They will teach you to keep asking, seeking and knocking until the door is opened to you.

My love, I want you to talk with Me about everything, because I desire fellowship with you. Learn to pray My will be done in every situation you face, as it is done is heaven, knowing that My will is perfect, because the plans I have for you are all good, and not for evil. I want you to know My love, that I Am always working all things together for your good, so pray My will, not your will, but My will be done.

My love, when you can't trace My hands; learn to trust My heart, knowing that I want what's best for you.

(Matt 6:9, 10; Jeremiah 29:11; Psalm 1119:49; 1Thess 5:17; Romans 8:28)

Love,

I Am your Divine Instructor

POINTS TO CONSIDER

1. Father wants you to begin your day with praise, worship, adoration, thanksgiving and prayer.

2. Learn to glorify His name as you begin your day.

3. Make Him priority number one in your life.

4. Pray the scriptures; they will give you hope, comfort, peace and joy for each day.

5. Be like the persistent widow, never give up, keep asking, seeking and knocking until the door opens.

6. Pray God's kingdom come and His will be done in every situation, knowing that His will is always best for you, remember His will is perfect.

7. Know that Papa always has your best interest at heart.

BE ENCOURAGED TODAY MY LOVE

My love,

I want you to know that My wisdom will give you patience, so if you lack wisdom please ask Me and I will give it to you, because I give liberally to all who ask. Please Know that I will not reject you for asking, as I give liberally to all those who ask of Me.

My love, My precious daughter, I want you to clothe yourself with compassion, kindness, humility, gentleness and patience, and remember Jesus who was your holy example displayed unlimited patience.

My love, I want you to exercise patience like the farmer who waits for the land to yield its valuable crops, and be reminded that I exercised patience with you so you can be saved.

I also want you to know My love that the example of true patience is suffering, so supplement your faith with a generous portion of moral excellence, and moral excellence with knowledge, and knowledge with self control, and self control with patient endurance, and godliness and brotherly affection for everyone.

(Proverbs 19:11;Eccl 7:12;Col3:12;1Tim1:16;2Tim4:2;James5:7;2Peter1:5&3:15; James 5:10)!

Love,

I Am your Patient Endurance

POINTS TO CONSIDER

1. When you use wisdom you will grow in patience.

2. Ask the Lord for wisdom, He will give you a bountiful supply, and He will not reject you for asking.

3. Father wants you to exercise patience with others just as He did with you.

4. Practice the golden rule; treat others the way you would like to be treated.

5. Be reminded that the example of true patience is suffering.

6. Exercise patient endurance and godliness with brotherly affection for everyone.

7. Exercise moral excellence.

BE ENCOURAGED TODAY MY LOVE

My love,

I want you to know that wrath is cruel and anger is outrageous, however, a soft answer diffuses strife. I also want you to know My love; that when you are slow to get angry you will carry a mark of honor, which will make you an excellent representative of Jesus Christ.

My Love, wrath is cruel and anger is outrageous; and angry women stirs up strife, so allow My love and peace to rule in your heart.

You also need to know that anger rests in the bosom of fools, so make the choice today to use the wisdom of the wise and be happy in Jesus name. Put anger far away from you, and cast all of your cares and concerns upon Me, knowing that I care deeply for you, and be reminded My love, that My word will instruct you in righteousness, and they will help you to understand so you can live right.

(Psalm 119:144; Proverbs 15:1,18&27:4;16:32, Colossians 3:17; Eccl 7:9),

Love,

I Am your Emotional Controller

POINTS TO CONSIDER

1. Father does not want you to be an angry quarrelsome person.

2. Know that a soft answer turns away wrath, it diffuses strife.

3. You also need to know that avoiding fights carries a mark of honor, and it makes you an excellent representative of Jesus Christ.

4. Allow the peace of the Lord to rule and reign in your heart.

5. Remember exercising self control is a fruit of the spirit.

6. Practice the presence of the Lord by reading, meditating and putting into practice what you have learned and you will have perfect peace.

7. Offer yourself as a living sacrifice to the Lord daily and He will keep your emotions under control.

♥BE ENCOURAGED TODAY MY LOVE♥

My love,

I want you to listen to My word, and treasure My instructions! Tune your ears to wisdom, and concentrate on understanding.

Cry out for insight, and ask for understanding. Search for them as you would for silver; and seek them like hidden treasures. Then you will understand what it means to fear Me, and you will gain knowledge of who I really Am. For I grant wisdom, and from My mouth comes knowledge and understanding.

My love, I grant treasures of common sense to the honest, and I Am a shield to all those who walk with integrity. I guard the paths of the just and protect those who are faithful to Me.

Be reminded My love, that I Am a faithful promise keeper. I want you to know that I rescue those who love Me and protect those who trust in My name (Proverbs 2:2-6&91:14-15)!

Love,

I Am your Treasure of Common Sense

POINTS TO CONSIDER

1. Listen to the voice of the Lord and treasure His instructions.

2. Seek Him for wisdom and understanding, and put it into practice for your life.

3. Seek the Lord for understanding and insight.

4. Love Him with all your heart, soul, mind and strength.

5. He wants you to gain knowledge of who He really is.

6. He is a Shield to all those who live a life of integrity.

7. You are guaranteed rescue and protection when you stay in love covenant with Him!

PRAY FOR AMERICA

Hear us, O Shepherd of Israel, you who lead Joseph like a flock; you who sit enthroned between the cherubim, shine forth. Restore us, O God; make your face shine upon us, that we may be saved.

Return to us, O God Almighty! Look down from heaven and see! Watch over this nation, humble your people, give us a desire to turn from all of our ways that displeases you, so you can hear us from heaven, forgive our sins and heal the land.

Father, remind your people that righteousness exalts a nation but sin is a reproach to any people. Lord, raise up more intercessors who would keep watch upon the walls so the enemy will not continue to have free rule and reign, give us leaders with integrity who will not continue to make the abominable practices of the people laws of the land.

Lord, I praise and thank you for those you have already planted and raised up for yourself, bless our leaders and all those you have placed in authority, may they be worthy of the calling you have placed upon their lives, I pray that they will have a heart of love for you, so they will love your people and do what's good, pure and lovely, and pleasing in your sight.

Lord, I praise and thank you for our President; let your hand rest upon him, and turn his heart in the direction for which you have purposed it to go. Open his ears so he can hear your voice clearly when you say; this is the way, walk in it!

Lord, revive us as a nation once again so people will begin to call on your name, while being reminded that you are holy and without holiness no one will see your face.

Restore us, O LORD God Almighty; make your face shine upon us, that we may be saved.

Father, I love you and I praise and thank you for hearing my prayers on behalf of this great nation which was founded upon your word. Thanks for granting my petition in Jesus Awesome, All Powerful Name. Amen!

(Psalm 80:1-3&14-18; 1Chronicles 7:14&15; Hebrews12:14)!

CONTACT INFORMATION

Min. Ingrid S. Rennie

301-459-7722

202-251-7751

Email address: *ingie@earthlink.net*

Webpage: *www.ingridrennie.vpweb.com*

FOR MORNING DEVOTION WITH INGRID VISIT:
WWW.BLOGTALKRADIO.COM/INGRIDS-TALK-SHOW